Ask Yourself This

A Daily Quotes & Questions Workbook
Featuring 366 Thoughts To Jump Start Your Mind Everyday

Workbook Complied By J Cleveland Payne

To Johanna Jasmine,
who finds new ways everyday
to remind me that it gets
harder and harder to keep up
if you don't keep moving.

And to Kristina,
who has pledged
to keep moving with me,
step by step,
as we try to keep up with
Johanna Jasmine.

Ask Yourself This: A Daily Quotes & Questions Workbook
Featuring 366 Thoughts To Jump Start Your Mind Everyday

I want to start out by thanking you for picking up and opening this book. I have no idea how you happened to come across it, but I am defiantly grateful that you have taken a moment to see what it is all about. This introduction will offer you a little insight into the books purpose, how it came to be in its current form, and how to get the most out of it.

The premise is simple: this book provides you a daily quote from various people. Some of the people were or are very famous, some of them were or are very powerful, and some of them will not be recognizable to you at all. Somehow, these people have managed to say or write (or become misinterpreted or misquoted) in some form of print with I have come across over the years. These quotes inspired a daily question that I used to jumpstart my mind every the morning by having to come up with an open and honest answer for the question myself.

In the past, Daily Quotes & Questions has been presented by me in print and online in various forms under various names. The last known form (at least as of the time of this printing) was a daily posting at the You Already Know The Answers website and blog, which you may or may not be able to find still online at http://youalreadyhavetheanswers.com. For the Answers Blog, I also shared a little of my thoughts on the daily question with the world as an often needed a jump start for newcomers to help them form answers of their own.

For this book presentation, I went back to the basics. Following the style and essence of my early quote and questions styled newsletter, I eliminated the outside influence from myself in the daily presentations, other than a hopefully subtle spin on the questions themselves. I wanted to emphasize that there is not a single right, wrong, or necessarily simple answer to any day's question. It's just your answer. That is the only rule you have to follow when coming up with your answer to the daily question. You don't even have to share it with anyone else if you don't want to. But as I work on my personal motto of 'getting the conversation started' between people, I would encourage you to share this book, and the daily quotes and questions inside of it, with other like-minded people. And if you are adventurous, go ahead and share it with a few not-so like-minded people that are willing to open up for some hypothetical dialog. The risk will be well worth it.

This book in its present form is the culmination of a lifetime of writing, over twenty years of personal improvement, and about 15 years of publishing variations of 'quotes of the day' in too many forms to remember. The evolution of this written delivery and the actual means of delivery (very helpful to be born in the current digital age and to have an early love of computers and the internet) is an interesting, although painfully embarrassing, study in my own personal growth.

One of the most important lessons I had to learn in my life was that it takes more than just a good idea to make your way to becoming a success. The original idea was producing a quote of the day, and through various stages of formatting, writing, rewriting, rereading later and reformatting and rewriting again, it took me years to find my personal groove and produce a product. Even one as simple as The Daily Quote & Question, which I could be completely proud of. Yet I kept having to produce sometimes sub-par, sometimes just plain awful products to figure out what would work and what would not. Often, life's distractions or just plain frustration got in the way of producing the newsletters daily. It would be that ping in the back of my head that would never let me completely let go of the idea of keeping it alive. When a free moment would arrive, I was back the keyboard to make the presentation a little better that is was the last go round. While the presentation in this book is a slightly different from the daily newsletter/blog posting that was last being produced, I have worked hard to ensure the work itself stands out as having extraordinary quality.

The format of the book is also simple: every page will be set for a date and will present that day's quote, that day's question, and some space that will enable you to use the book as a personal journal that you can easily refer to in the future. The journal aspect is key. I have a thought attached to every blog posting of the Daily Quote & Question that shows what I was thinking when I was writing the question from the quote that inspired it. Having a running log of how you answered the daily questions that you can review after the fact offers a look back at yourself a particular point in time. Reread a question later in your life, whether it happened to be a few weeks to a few decades later, and I will guarantee some added life experience will change your perspective and your answer.

It's a simple book with a simple mission, and I know you will enjoy embarking on that mission day by day, question by question, as you get an early mental boost that will extend until a clearer and more open view of the world around you, along with the world inside you.

Once again, I want to thank you for picking up and opening this book. You've made an excellent choice.

- J Cleveland Payne

Ask Yourself This

A Daily Quotes & Questions Workbook

Featuring 366 Thoughts To Jump Start Your Mind Everyday

JANUARY

Today's Quote: "Never make a defense or an apology until you are accused." - King Charles I of England

Today's Question: Is it truly easier to get forgiveness than permission?

_____

_____

_____

_____

_____

_____

_____

_____

_____

_____

_____

_____

_____

_____

_____

_____

_____

Today's Quote: "People might not get all they work for in this world, but they must certainly work for all they get." - Frederick Douglass

Today's Question: If all your dreams could be fulfilled in an instant, would you accept them?

_____

_____

_____

_____

_____

_____

_____

_____

_____

_____

_____

_____

_____

_____

_____

_____

_____

Today's Quote: "The pleasure of love is in loving." - Francois de La
Rochefoucauld

Today's Question: Are you able to give as much love as you receive?

_____

_____

_____

_____

_____

_____

_____

_____

_____

_____

_____

_____

_____

_____

_____

_____

_____

_____

_____

Today's Quote: "It is a waste of energy to be angry with a man who behaves badly, just as it is to be angry with a car that won't go." - Bertrand Russell

Today's Question: Is your anger focused in the right direction?

_____

_____

_____

_____

_____

_____

_____

_____

_____

_____

_____

_____

_____

_____

_____

_____

_____

_____

Today's Quote: "Man's mind, once stretched by a new idea, never regains its original dimensions." - Oliver Wendell Holmes

Today's Question: What is keeping you from facing the fear of the unknown?

_____

_____

_____

_____

_____

_____

_____

_____

_____

_____

_____

_____

_____

_____

_____

_____

_____

January 6th

Today's Quote: "It is impossible to defeat an ignorant man in argument." - William G. McAdoo

Today's Question: How do you deal with someone who chooses to remain ignorant, despite facing the truth?

_____

_____

_____

_____

_____

_____

_____

_____

_____

_____

_____

_____

_____

_____

_____

_____

Today's Quote: "Though I am not naturally honest, I am so sometimes by chance." - William Shakespeare

Today's Question: Are you as honest with others as you are with yourself?

_____

_____

_____

_____

_____

_____

_____

_____

_____

_____

_____

_____

_____

_____

_____

_____

_____

Today's Quote: "Politeness and consideration for others is like investing pennies and getting dollars back." - Thomas Sowell

Today's Question: Are you minding your manners?

_____

_____

_____

_____

_____

_____

_____

_____

_____

_____

_____

_____

_____

_____

_____

_____

_____

_____

January 9th

Today's Quote: "I told my psychiatrist that everyone hates me. He said I was being ridiculous - everyone hasn't met me yet." - Rodney Dangerfield

Today's Question: How much of your worry is unwarranted?

_____

_____

_____

_____

_____

_____

_____

_____

_____

_____

_____

_____

_____

_____

_____

_____

_____

_____

Today's Quote: "Sanity calms, but madness is more interesting." - John Russell

Today's Question: Are you making your life more boring on purpose?

_____

_____

_____

_____

_____

_____

_____

_____

_____

_____

_____

_____

_____

_____

_____

_____

_____

Today's Quote: "An idealist is one who, on noticing that a rose smells better than a cabbage, concludes that it will also make better soup." - H. L. Mencken

Today's Question: Do you let assumptions drive you to false conclusions?

_____

_____

_____

_____

_____

_____

_____

_____

_____

_____

_____

_____

_____

_____

_____

_____

_____

_____

January 12th

Today's Quote: "To avoid situations in which you might make mistakes may be the biggest mistake of all." - Peter McWilliams

Today's Question: Do you use your mistakes as a learning tool or as reason to give up?

_____

_____

_____

_____

_____

_____

_____

_____

_____

_____

_____

_____

_____

_____

_____

_____

_____

_____

Today's Quote: "Don't worry about people stealing an idea. If it's original, you will have to ram it down their throats." - Howard Aiken

Today's Question: Today's Question: Do you find it hard to sell the idea of making changes to other people?

_____

_____

_____

_____

_____

_____

_____

_____

_____

_____

_____

_____

_____

_____

_____

_____

_____

_____

Today's Quote: "I'm all in favor of keeping dangerous weapons out of the hands of fools. Let's start with typewriters." - Solomon Short

Today's Question: Are the words you use a source of hurt or a source of healing?

_____

_____

_____

_____

_____

_____

_____

_____

_____

_____

_____

_____

_____

_____

_____

_____

_____

Today's Quote: "I didn't really say everything I said." - Yogi Berra

Today's Question: What are you falsely getting credit or blame for?

_____

_____

_____

_____

_____

_____

_____

_____

_____

_____

_____

_____

_____

_____

_____

_____

_____

_____

_____

Today's Quote: "Youth is a wonderful thing. What a crime to waste it on children." - George Bernard Shaw

Today's Question: Would you take a chance at reliving your youth?

_____

_____

_____

_____

_____

_____

_____

_____

_____

_____

_____

_____

_____

_____

_____

_____

_____

_____

January 17ᵗʰ

Today's Quote: "Sit down before fact as a little child, be prepared to give up every preconceived notion . . . or you shall learn nothing." - Thomas H. Huxley

Today's Question: Are you really open to learning?

_____

_____

_____

_____

_____

_____

_____

_____

_____

_____

_____

_____

_____

_____

_____

_____

_____

_____

Today's Quote: When a thing is done, it's done. Don't look back. Look forward to your next objective." - George C. Marshall

Today's Question: Why can't you let go?

_____

_____

_____

_____

_____

_____

_____

_____

_____

_____

_____

_____

_____

_____

_____

_____

_____

_____

Today's Quote: "While it's important to win, it's imperative to compete." - David Weinbaum

Today's Question: How important is it for you to finish the race, even when you have no chance of winning?

_____

_____

_____

_____

_____

_____

_____

_____

_____

_____

_____

_____

_____

_____

_____

_____

_____

Today's Quote: "He who asks is a fool for five minutes, but he who does not ask remains a fool forever" - Chinese Proverb

Today's Question: Why are you afraid to ask for what you want?

_____

_____

_____

_____

_____

_____

_____

_____

_____

_____

_____

_____

_____

_____

_____

_____

_____

Today's Quote: "The one thing more difficult than following a regimen is not imposing it on others." - Marcel Proust

Today's Question: Are the people you want to take on your journey with you ready?

_____

_____

_____

_____

_____

_____

_____

_____

_____

_____

_____

_____

_____

_____

_____

_____

_____

_____

Today's Quote: "If you want creative workers, give them enough time to play." - John Cleese

Today's Question: Do you get enough play time in your day?

_____

_____

_____

_____

_____

_____

_____

_____

_____

_____

_____

_____

_____

_____

_____

_____

_____

Today's Quote: "If you think you can do a thing or think you can't do a thing, you're right." - Henry Ford

Today's Question: How much faith do you have in yourself?

_____

_____

_____

_____

_____

_____

_____

_____

_____

_____

_____

_____

_____

_____

_____

_____

_____

Today's Quote: "If we take care of the moments, the years will take care of themselves." - Maria Edgeworth

Today's Question: Are you so focused on future that you can't see life in the moment?

_____

_____

_____

_____

_____

_____

_____

_____

_____

_____

_____

_____

_____

_____

_____

_____

January 25th

Today's Quote: "You must learn from the mistakes of others. You can't possibly live long enough to make them all yourself." - Sam Levenson

Today's Question: What can you learn from studying the successes and failures of those who have walked the path ahead of you?

_____

_____

_____

_____

_____

_____

_____

_____

_____

_____

_____

_____

_____

_____

_____

_____

_____

_____

Today's Quote: "Man invented language to satisfy his deep need to complain." - Lily Tomlin

Today's Question: Why not just fix the problem rather than complain about it?

_____

_____

_____

_____

_____

_____

_____

_____

_____

_____

_____

_____

_____

_____

_____

_____

_____

Today's Quote: "People seem not to see that their opinion of the world is also a confession of their character." - Ralph Waldo Emerson

Today's Question: Can a change of view bring a change in your character?

_____

_____

_____

_____

_____

_____

_____

_____

_____

_____

_____

_____

_____

_____

_____

_____

_____

Today's Quote: "Men are not against you; they are merely for themselves."
- Gene Fowler

Today's Question: Are you a selfless person?

_____

_____

_____

_____

_____

_____

_____

_____

_____

_____

_____

_____

_____

_____

_____

_____

_____

_____

Today's Quote: "You better live your best and act your best and think your best today, for today is the sure preparation for tomorrow and all the other tomorrows that follow." - Harriet Martineau

Today's Question: Are you doing enough to prepare for tomorrow?

_____

_____

_____

_____

_____

_____

_____

_____

_____

_____

_____

_____

_____

_____

_____

_____

_____

_____

_____

Today's Quote: "You can fool some of the people all of the time, and all of the people some of the time, but you can not fool all of the people all of the time." - Abraham Lincoln

Today's Question: Who are you trying to fool?

_____

_____

_____

_____

_____

_____

_____

_____

_____

_____

_____

_____

_____

_____

_____

_____

_____

_____

January 31st

Today's Quote: "The price one pays for pursuing any profession or calling is an intimate knowledge of its ugly side." - James Baldwin

Today's Question: Are there some not-so-positive aspects of your pursuits?

_____

_____

_____

_____

_____

_____

_____

_____

_____

_____

_____

_____

_____

_____

_____

_____

_____

_____

FEBRUARY

Today's Quote: "People who ask our advice almost never take it. Yet we should never refuse to give it, upon request, for it often helps us to see our own way more clearly." - Brendan Francis

Today's Question: Do you take the advice you ask for?

_____

_____

_____

_____

_____

_____

_____

_____

_____

_____

_____

_____

_____

_____

_____

_____

_____

Today's Quote: "Realize that if you have time to whine and complain about something then you have the time to do something about it." - Anthony J. D'Angelo

Today's Question: Is whining your weapon of choice for getting your way?

_____

_____

_____

_____

_____

_____

_____

_____

_____

_____

_____

_____

_____

_____

_____

_____

_____

Today's Quote: "Unless commitment is made, there are only promises and hopes . . . but no plans." - Peter Drucker

Today's Question: Are you truly committed to the cause?

_____

_____

_____

_____

_____

_____

_____

_____

_____

_____

_____

_____

_____

_____

_____

_____

_____

_____

Today's Quote: "One of the advantages of being disorderly is that one is constantly making exciting discoveries." - A. A. Milne

Today's Question: What new discoveries are you making in the midst of the chaos in your life?

_____

_____

_____

_____

_____

_____

_____

_____

_____

_____

_____

_____

_____

_____

_____

Today's Quote: "Everywhere I go I find a poet has been there before me." - Sigmund Freud

Today's Question: Can you handle the life of a trailblazer?

_____

_____

_____

_____

_____

_____

_____

_____

_____

_____

_____

_____

_____

_____

_____

_____

_____

_____

Today's Quote: "The trees that are slow to grow bear the best fruit." - Moliere

Today's Question: Do you have the ability to wait until the right moment to act?

_____

_____

_____

_____

_____

_____

_____

_____

_____

_____

_____

_____

_____

_____

_____

Today's Quote: "Believe in life! Always human beings will live and progress to greater, broader and fuller life." - W. E. B. Du Bois

Today's Question: Do you cherish, respect, and celebrate life?

_____

_____

_____

_____

_____

_____

_____

_____

_____

_____

_____

_____

_____

_____

_____

_____

_____

February 8th

Today's Quote: "A person is always startled when he hears himself seriously called an old man for the first time." - Oliver Wendell Holmes

Today's Question: Are you old by age or by mentality?

_____

_____

_____

_____

_____

_____

_____

_____

_____

_____

_____

_____

_____

_____

_____

_____

Today's Quote: "Planning is a real waste of time . . . for those who waste time." - Doug Firebaugh

Today's Question: Do you take the time to properly plan out your projects?

_____

_____

_____

_____

_____

_____

_____

_____

_____

_____

_____

_____

_____

_____

_____

_____

_____

Today's Quote: "I have left orders to be awakened at any time in case of national emergency, even if I'm in a cabinet meeting." - Ronald Reagan

Today's Question: How much of your time is spent sleeping through daily events?

_____

_____

_____

_____

_____

_____

_____

_____

_____

_____

_____

_____

_____

_____

_____

_____

Today's Quote: "A lawyer starts life giving $500 worth of law for $5 and ends giving $5 worth for $500." - Benjamin H. Brewster

Today's Question: What is your advice worth?

_____

_____

_____

_____

_____

_____

_____

_____

_____

_____

_____

_____

_____

_____

_____

_____

Today's Quote: "We all have big changes in our lives that are more or less a second chance." - Harrison Ford

Today's Question: Do you give second chances to those who deserve them?

_____

_____

_____

_____

_____

_____

_____

_____

_____

_____

_____

_____

_____

_____

_____

_____

_____

February 13th

Today's Quote: "Do not fear death so much, but rather the inadequate life."
- Bertolt Brecht

Today's Question: Are you proud of the life you are living?

_____

_____

_____

_____

_____

_____

_____

_____

_____

_____

_____

_____

_____

_____

_____

_____

_____

Today's Quote: "If your daily life seems poor, do not blame it; blame yourself, tell yourself that you are not poet enough to call forth its riches." - Rainer Maria Rilke

Today's Question: Do you blame the circumstances of your life for leading you to where you are?

_____

_____

_____

_____

_____

_____

_____

_____

_____

_____

_____

_____

_____

_____

_____

_____

_____

Today's Quote: "We are an impossibility in an impossible universe." - Ray Bradbury

Today's Question: How much of your life is spent attempting the impossible?

_____

_____

_____

_____

_____

_____

_____

_____

_____

_____

_____

_____

_____

_____

_____

_____

Today's Quote: "Guilt is anger directed at ourselves--at what we did or did not do." - Peter McWilliams

Today's Question: Is guilt keeping you from putting forth your best?

_____

_____

_____

_____

_____

_____

_____

_____

_____

_____

_____

_____

_____

_____

_____

Today's Quote: "We must use time as a tool, not as a crutch." - John F. Kennedy

Today's Question: Do you see time as an asset or a liability?

_____

_____

_____

_____

_____

_____

_____

_____

_____

_____

_____

_____

_____

_____

_____

_____

_____

_____

February 18th

Today's Quote: "A fellow who is always declaring he's no fool usually has his suspicions." - Wilson Mizner

Today's Question: Are you fooling yourself?

_____

_____

_____

_____

_____

_____

_____

_____

_____

_____

_____

_____

_____

_____

_____

_____

_____

Today's Quote: "Your chances of success are directly proportional to the degree of pleasure you derive from what you do." - Michael Korda

Today's Question: What aspects of your pursuits bring joy, and what aspects bring pain?

_____

_____

_____

_____

_____

_____

_____

_____

_____

_____

_____

_____

_____

_____

_____

_____

_____

Today's Quote: "The only place where success comes before work is a dictionary." - Vidal Sassoon

Today's Question: Would you appreciate success any less if it was just handed to you?

_____

_____

_____

_____

_____

_____

_____

_____

_____

_____

_____

_____

_____

_____

_____

_____

Today's Quote: "Please give me some good advice in your next letter. I promise not to follow it." - Edna St. Vincent Millay

Today's Question: Did you follow other's advice?

_____

_____

_____

_____

_____

_____

_____

_____

_____

_____

_____

_____

_____

_____

_____

_____

_____

_____

Today's Quote: "Opportunity is missed by most people because it is dressed in overalls and looks like work." - Thomas A. Edison

Today's Question: Do you run from potential opportunities because of the fear of having to take on a heavier workload?

_____

_____

_____

_____

_____

_____

_____

_____

_____

_____

_____

_____

_____

_____

_____

_____

_____

Today's Quote: "Reality is merely an illusion, albeit a very persistent one." - Albert Einstein

Today's Question: Can you disbelieve yourself to a new reality?

_____

_____

_____

_____

_____

_____

_____

_____

_____

_____

_____

_____

_____

_____

_____

_____

_____

_____

Today's Quote: "Worry is a misuse of imagination." - Dan Zadra

Today's Question: What changes in your life would help relieve you of your worries?

_____

_____

_____

_____

_____

_____

_____

_____

_____

_____

_____

_____

_____

_____

_____

_____

_____

Today's Quote: "History will be kind to me for I intend to write it." - Sir Winston Churchill

Today's Topic For Reflection: Will you be the one to write your own history?

_____

_____

_____

_____

_____

_____

_____

_____

_____

_____

_____

_____

_____

_____

_____

_____

_____

Today's Quote: "It is difficult to produce a television documentary that is both incisive and probing when every twelve minutes one is interrupted by twelve dancing rabbits singing about toilet paper." - Rod Serling

Today's Question: What would it take to eliminate some of the interruptions in your life that keep you off track?

_____

_____

_____

_____

_____

_____

_____

_____

_____

_____

_____

_____

_____

_____

_____

_____

_____

Today's Quote: "Formulate and stamp indelibly on your mind a mental picture of yourself as succeeding. Hold this picture tenaciously. Never permit it to fade. Your mind will seek to develop the picture . . . Do not build up obstacles in your imagination." - Norman Vincent Peale

Today's Question: Can a mental picture of success really lead you to succeed?

_____

_____

_____

_____

_____

_____

_____

_____

_____

_____

_____

_____

_____

_____

_____

_____

Today's Quote: "The chief lesson I have learned in a long life is that the only way to make a man trustworthy is to trust him; and the surest way to make him untrustworthy is to distrust him and show your distrust." - Henry L. Stimson

Today's Question: How much trust do you put in others?

_____

_____

_____

_____

_____

_____

_____

_____

_____

_____

_____

_____

_____

_____

Today's Quote: "The only factor becoming scarce in a world of abundance is human attention." - Kevin Kelly

Today's Question: Can you so much that it can diminish a good situation?

_____

_____

_____

_____

_____

_____

_____

_____

_____

_____

_____

_____

_____

_____

_____

_____

MARCH

March 1st

Today's Quote: "Some are kissing mothers and some are scolding mothers, but it is love just the same." - Pearl S. Buck

Today's Question: How do you show your loved ones that they are truly loved?

_____

_____

_____

_____

_____

_____

_____

_____

_____

_____

_____

_____

_____

_____

_____

_____

Today's Quote: "If an idea's worth having once, it's worth having twice." - Tom Stoppard

Today's Question: Do you fear not having enough good ideas?

_____

_____

_____

_____

_____

_____

_____

_____

_____

_____

_____

_____

_____

_____

_____

_____

_____

_____

March 3rd

Today's Quote: "When you can't have what you want, it's time to start wanting what you have." - Kathleen A. Sutton

Today's Question: Do you constantly want more?

_____

_____

_____

_____

_____

_____

_____

_____

_____

_____

_____

_____

_____

_____

_____

_____

_____

Today's Quote: "Waste no more time talking about great souls and how they should be. Become one yourself!" - Marcus Aurelius

Today's Question: How much of your pursuit is pure lip service?

_____

_____

_____

_____

_____

_____

_____

_____

_____

_____

_____

_____

_____

_____

_____

_____

_____

_____

Today's Quote: "It is by the goodness of God that in our country we have those three unspeakably precious things: freedom of speech, freedom of conscience, and the prudence never to practice either of them." - Mark Twain

Today's Question: Are you a slave to your own freedom?

_____

_____

_____

_____

_____

_____

_____

_____

_____

_____

_____

_____

_____

_____

_____

_____

Today's Quote: "Sometimes I worry about being a success in a mediocre world." - Lily Tomlin

Today's Question: Are you being fair to yourself if you don't put forth your best efforts?

_____

_____

_____

_____

_____

_____

_____

_____

_____

_____

_____

_____

_____

_____

_____

_____

Today's Quote: "Nearly all men can stand adversity, but if you want to test a man's character, give him power." - Abraham Lincoln

Today's Question: Are you ready for the real test?

_____

_____

_____

_____

_____

_____

_____

_____

_____

_____

_____

_____

_____

_____

_____

_____

_____

Today's Quote: "Take calculated risks. That is quite different from being rash." - George S. Patton

Today's Question: When do you decide the cost is worth the risk?

_____

_____

_____

_____

_____

_____

_____

_____

_____

_____

_____

_____

_____

_____

_____

_____

_____

_____

Today's Quote: "What you do speaks so loud that I cannot hear what you say." - Ralph Waldo Emerson

Today's Question: How much louder are your actions speaking than your words?

_____

_____

_____

_____

_____

_____

_____

_____

_____

_____

_____

_____

_____

_____

_____

_____

_____

_____

Today's Quote: "Some things have to be believed to be seen." - Ralph Hodgson

Today's Question: Do you truly believe your dreams will come true?

_____

_____

_____

_____

_____

_____

_____

_____

_____

_____

_____

_____

_____

_____

_____

_____

_____

_____

Today's Quote: "Wait until it is night before saying that it has been a fine day." - French Proverb

Today's Question: Do you tend to claim victory before the battle has been fought?

_____

_____

_____

_____

_____

_____

_____

_____

_____

_____

_____

_____

_____

_____

_____

_____

Today's Quote: "Be master of your petty annoyances and conserve your energies for the big, worthwhile things. It isn't the mountain ahead that wears you out--it's the grain of sand in your shoe." - Robert Service

Today's Question: Are the little problems wearing you down?

_____

_____

_____

_____

_____

_____

_____

_____

_____

_____

_____

_____

_____

_____

_____

_____

_____

Today's Quote: "Money is better than poverty, if only for financial reasons."
- Woody Allen

Today's Question: Are your views on money tied into your emotions?

_____

_____

_____

_____

_____

_____

_____

_____

_____

_____

_____

_____

_____

_____

_____

_____

_____

_____

_____

Today's Quote: "Know the true value of time; snatch, seize, and enjoy every moment of it. No idleness; no laziness; no procrastination; never put off till tomorrow what you can do today." - Lord Chesterfield

Today's Question: Are you making the best use of your time?

_____

_____

_____

_____

_____

_____

_____

_____

_____

_____

_____

_____

_____

_____

_____

_____

_____

_____

Today's Quote: "Today I will do what others won't, so tomorrow I can accomplish what others can't." - Jerry Rice

Today's Question: What can you do today to give yourself an advantage in the future?

_____

_____

_____

_____

_____

_____

_____

_____

_____

_____

_____

_____

_____

_____

_____

_____

_____

Today's Quote: "Courage is being scared to death - but saddling up anyway." - John Wayne

Today's Question: What do you need to keep a significant fear from holding you back?

_____

_____

_____

_____

_____

_____

_____

_____

_____

_____

_____

_____

_____

_____

_____

_____

March 17th

Today's Quote: "Make rest a necessity, not an objective. Only rest long enough to gather strength." - Jim Rohn

Today's Question: Is rest something that recharges you or drains you?

_____

_____

_____

_____

_____

_____

_____

_____

_____

_____

_____

_____

_____

_____

_____

_____

_____

_____

_____

Today's Quote: "Nothing is said that has not been said before." - Terence

Today's Question: What is your favorite exercise in futility?

_____

_____

_____

_____

_____

_____

_____

_____

_____

_____

_____

_____

_____

_____

_____

_____

_____

_____

Today's Quote: "Under all speech that is good for anything there lies a silence that is better. Silence is deep as Eternity; speech is shallow as Time." - Thomas Carlyle

Today's Question: What does your silence say about you?

_____

_____

_____

_____

_____

_____

_____

_____

_____

_____

_____

_____

_____

_____

_____

_____

_____

_____

Today's Quote: "Nothing ever goes away." - Barry Commoner

Today's Question: Is there something you wish you could take back?

_____

_____

_____

_____

_____

_____

_____

_____

_____

_____

_____

_____

_____

_____

_____

_____

_____

_____

_____

_____

_____

March 21st

Today's Quote: "Life is a long lesson in humility." - James M. Barrie

Today's Question: What life lesson has taught you the most so far?

_____

_____

_____

_____

_____

_____

_____

_____

_____

_____

_____

_____

_____

_____

_____

_____

_____

_____

_____

Today's Quote: "We're here for a reason. I believe a bit of the reason is to throw little torches out to lead people through the dark." - Whoopi Goldberg

Today's Question: Why are you here?

_____

_____

_____

_____

_____

_____

_____

_____

_____

_____

_____

_____

_____

_____

_____

_____

_____

Today's Quote: "I'm an artist who is a Christian. I'm not a Christian artist." - Johnny Cash

Today's Question: How do you keep other people from labeling you?

_____

_____

_____

_____

_____

_____

_____

_____

_____

_____

_____

_____

_____

_____

_____

_____

_____

_____

Today's Quote: "Do not spoil what you have by desiring what you have not; but remember that what you now have was once among the things you only hoped for." - Epicurus

Today's Question: Why would you want what you haven't got?

_____

_____

_____

_____

_____

_____

_____

_____

_____

_____

_____

_____

_____

_____

_____

_____

_____

_____

_____

Today's Quote: "One never notices what has been done; one can only see what remains to be done." - Marie Curie

Today's Question: When you act, does anyone notice?

_____

_____

_____

_____

_____

_____

_____

_____

_____

_____

_____

_____

_____

_____

_____

_____

_____

_____

Today's Quote: "Music with dinner is an insult both to the cook and the violinist." - G. K. Chesterton

Today's Question: How well do you multitask?

_____

_____

_____

_____

_____

_____

_____

_____

_____

_____

_____

_____

_____

_____

_____

_____

_____

_____

Today's Quote: "Sometimes when you look in his eyes you get the feeling that someone else is driving." - David Letterman

Today's Question: Are you really in control?

_____

_____

_____

_____

_____

_____

_____

_____

_____

_____

_____

_____

_____

_____

_____

_____

_____

Today's Quote: "Look to your health; and if you have it, praise God and value it next to conscience; for health is the second blessing that we mortals are capable of, a blessing money can't buy." - Izaak Walton

Today's Question: Would you choose health or wealth?

_____

_____

_____

_____

_____

_____

_____

_____

_____

_____

_____

_____

_____

_____

_____

_____

_____

_____

March 29th

Today's Quote: "Honest differences are often a healthy sign of progress." - Mahatma Gandhi

Today's Question: How well do you argue?

_____

_____

_____

_____

_____

_____

_____

_____

_____

_____

_____

_____

_____

_____

_____

_____

Today's Quote: "The only way to get rid of a temptation is to yield to it. Resist it, and your soul grows sick with longing for the things it has forbidden to itself." - Oscar Wilde

Today's Question: Is there a good time to give into temptation?

_____

_____

_____

_____

_____

_____

_____

_____

_____

_____

_____

_____

_____

_____

_____

_____

_____

_____

Today's Quote: "Traditions are the guideposts driven deep in our subconscious minds. The most powerful ones are those we can't even describe, aren't even aware of." - Ellen Goodman

Today's Question: What is your favorite tradition?

_____

_____

_____

_____

_____

_____

_____

_____

_____

_____

_____

_____

_____

_____

_____

_____

_____

APRIL

Today's Quote: "To argue with a person who has renounced the use of reason is like administering medicine to the dead." - Thomas Paine

Today's Question: Are you supporting your argument with words out of context?

_____

_____

_____

_____

_____

_____

_____

_____

_____

_____

_____

_____

_____

_____

_____

_____

_____

_____

April 2nd

Today's Quote: "Basic research is what I am doing when I don't know what I am doing." - Wernher von Braun

Today's Question: What is your favorite excuse?

_____

_____

_____

_____

_____

_____

_____

_____

_____

_____

_____

_____

_____

_____

_____

_____

_____

Today's Quote: "Now and then an innocent man is sent to the legislature." - Kin Hubbard

Today's Question: Have you ever purposely led another person astray?

_____

_____

_____

_____

_____

_____

_____

_____

_____

_____

_____

_____

_____

_____

_____

_____

_____

_____

_____

Today's Quote: "Only the curious will learn and only the resolute overcome the obstacles to learning. The quest quotient has always excited me more than the intelligence quotient." - Eugene S. Wilson

Today's Question: What lesson cost you the most to learn?

_____

_____

_____

_____

_____

_____

_____

_____

_____

_____

_____

_____

_____

_____

_____

_____

_____

_____

_____

Today's Quote: "No one who has read official documents needs to be told how easy it is to conceal the essential truth under the apparently candid and all- disclosing phrases of a voluminous and particularizing report . . ." - Woodrow Wilson

Today's Question: How hard is it to hide a lie inside of the apparent truth?

_____

_____

_____

_____

_____

_____

_____

_____

_____

_____

_____

_____

_____

_____

_____

_____

_____

Today's Quote: "He who hesitates is a damned fool." - Mae West

Today's Question: What are you waiting for?

_____

_____

_____

_____

_____

_____

_____

_____

_____

_____

_____

_____

_____

_____

_____

_____

_____

_____

April 7th

Today's Quote: "I would rather try to persuade a man to go along, because once I have persuaded him he will stick. If I scare him, he will stay just as long as he is scared, and then he is gone." - Dwight D. Eisenhower

Today's Question: Why are you going along for the ride?

_____

_____

_____

_____

_____

_____

_____

_____

_____

_____

_____

_____

_____

_____

_____

_____

_____

_____

Today's Quote: "The farther behind I leave the past, the closer I am to forging my own character." - Isabelle Eberhardt

Today's Question: What has made your life better now that you have left it behind?

_____

_____

_____

_____

_____

_____

_____

_____

_____

_____

_____

_____

_____

_____

_____

_____

_____

_____

_____

Today's Quote: "Success is liking yourself, liking what you do, and liking how you do it." - Maya Angelou

Today's Question: Do you like what you do?

_____

_____

_____

_____

_____

_____

_____

_____

_____

_____

_____

_____

_____

_____

_____

_____

_____

April 10th

Today's Quote: "The man who wants to lead the orchestra must turn his back on the crowd." - James Crook

Today's Question: Are you leading for the right reasons?

_____

_____

_____

_____

_____

_____

_____

_____

_____

_____

_____

_____

_____

_____

_____

_____

_____

_____

Today's Quote: "Never again clutter your days or nights with so many menial and unimportant things that you have no time to accept a real challenge when it comes along. This applies to play as well as work. A day merely survived is no cause for celebration. You are not here to fritter away your precious hours when you have the ability to accomplish so much by making a slight change in your routine. No more busy work. No more hiding from success. Leave time, leave space, to grow. Now. Now! Not tomorrow!"
- Og Mandino

Today's Question: Is starting a new routine a challenge or a chore?

_____

_____

_____

_____

_____

_____

_____

_____

_____

_____

_____

_____

_____

_____

_____

Today's Quote: "People who say they're not interested in money will lie about other things too." - Zig Ziglar

Today's Question: What is the truth?

_____

_____

_____

_____

_____

_____

_____

_____

_____

_____

_____

_____

_____

_____

_____

_____

_____

Today's Quote: "A man thinks that by mouthing hard words he understands hard things." - Herman Melville

Today's Question: Are the words you speak doing harm to yourself or others?

_____

_____

_____

_____

_____

_____

_____

_____

_____

_____

_____

_____

_____

_____

_____

_____

_____

Today's Quote: "If what they say is "Nothing is forever," then what makes love the exception?" - 'André 3000' Benjamin

Today's Question: What would you really want to last forever?

_____

_____

_____

_____

_____

_____

_____

_____

_____

_____

_____

_____

_____

_____

_____

_____

_____

_____

_____

Today's Quote: "I believe in looking reality straight in the eye and denying it." - Garrison Keillor

Today's Question: When has denial actually worked to your benefit?

_____

_____

_____

_____

_____

_____

_____

_____

_____

_____

_____

_____

_____

_____

_____

_____

_____

_____

Today's Quote: "I will follow the right side even to the fire, but excluding the fire if I can." - Michel de Montaigne

Today's Question: Just how far are you willing to go?

_____

_____

_____

_____

_____

_____

_____

_____

_____

_____

_____

_____

_____

_____

_____

_____

_____

_____

_____

_____

Today's Quote: "Hegel was right when he said that we learn from history that man can never learn anything from history." - George Bernard Shaw

Today's Question: How often do you review your past to plot your future?

_____

_____

_____

_____

_____

_____

_____

_____

_____

_____

_____

_____

_____

_____

_____

_____

_____

_____

_____

Today's Quote: "Where is there dignity unless there is honesty?" - Cicero

Today's Question: Isn't about time you were honest with yourself?

_____

_____

_____

_____

_____

_____

_____

_____

_____

_____

_____

_____

_____

_____

_____

_____

_____

_____

_____

_____

Today's Quote: "I was brought up to believe that how I saw myself was more important than how others saw me." - Anwar el-Sadat

Today's Question: How do you see yourself?

_____

_____

_____

_____

_____

_____

_____

_____

_____

_____

_____

_____

_____

_____

_____

_____

_____

_____

Today's Quote: "The discovery of a new dish does more for human happiness than the discovery of a new star." - Anthelme Brillat-Savarin

Today's Question: What little discovery has meant the most to your life?

_____

_____

_____

_____

_____

_____

_____

_____

_____

_____

_____

_____

_____

_____

_____

_____

_____

_____

Today's Quote: "What does it matter how one comes by the truth so long as one pounces upon it and lives by it?" - Henry Miller

Today's Question: Do you live the truth?

_____

_____

_____

_____

_____

_____

_____

_____

_____

_____

_____

_____

_____

_____

_____

_____

_____

_____

April 22nd

Today's Quote: "An ounce of loyalty is worth a pound of cleverness." - Elbert Hubbard

Today's Question: To whom or what do your loyalties lie?

_____

_____

_____

_____

_____

_____

_____

_____

_____

_____

_____

_____

_____

_____

_____

_____

_____

_____

April 23rd

Today's Quote: "The only reason I made a commercial for American Express was to pay for my American Express bill." - Peter Ustinov

Today's Question: How do you rationalize your actions?

_____

_____

_____

_____

_____

_____

_____

_____

_____

_____

_____

_____

_____

_____

_____

_____

April 24th

Today's Quote: "Posterity is as likely to be wrong as anyone else." - Heywood Broun

Today's Question: Can you admit when you are wrong?

_____

_____

_____

_____

_____

_____

_____

_____

_____

_____

_____

_____

_____

_____

_____

_____

_____

_____

April 25th

Today's Quote: "We must be willing to get rid of the life we've planned, so as to have the life that is waiting for us." - Joseph Campbell

Today's Question: What have you traded to improve your life?

_____

_____

_____

_____

_____

_____

_____

_____

_____

_____

_____

_____

_____

_____

_____

_____

_____

_____

Today's Quote: "Listen to the whispers and you won't have to hear the screams." - Cherokee Saying

Today's Question: Do you ignore the warning signs?

_____

_____

_____

_____

_____

_____

_____

_____

_____

_____

_____

_____

_____

_____

_____

_____

_____

Today's Quote: "Procrastination isn't the problem, it's the solution. So procrastinate now, don't put it off." - Ellen DeGeneres

Today's Question: Are you applying the right solutions to your problems?

_____

_____

_____

_____

_____

_____

_____

_____

_____

_____

_____

_____

_____

_____

_____

_____

_____

_____

Today's Quote: "Knowledge is of two kinds. We know a subject ourselves, or we know where we can find information on it." - Samuel Johnson

Today's Question: Do you have a brain trust?

April 29th

Today's Quote: "I was always taught to respect my elders and I've now reached the age when I don't have anybody to respect." - George Burns

Today's Question: Are you gaining wisdom as you grow older?

_____

_____

_____

_____

_____

_____

_____

_____

_____

_____

_____

_____

_____

_____

_____

_____

_____

_____

Today's Quote: "Good judgment comes from experience. Experience comes from bad judgment." - Unknown

Today's Question: Are you experienced?

_____

_____

_____

_____

_____

_____

_____

_____

_____

_____

_____

_____

_____

_____

_____

_____

_____

_____

_____

_____

MAY

Today's Quote: "The important thing is this: To be able at any moment to sacrifice what we are for what we could become." - Charles DuBois

Today's Question: Are you so attached to an old way that it impedes trying new ways?

_____

_____

_____

_____

_____

_____

_____

_____

_____

_____

_____

_____

_____

_____

_____

_____

_____

_____

Today's Quote: "I hate quotations. Tell me what you know." - Ralph Waldo Emerson

Today's Question: Do you work better when you already have the answers?

_____

_____

_____

_____

_____

_____

_____

_____

_____

_____

_____

_____

_____

_____

_____

_____

_____

_____

Today's Quote: "I think that somehow, we learn who we really are and then live with that decision." - Eleanor Roosevelt

Today's Question: Do you like who you are?

_____

_____

_____

_____

_____

_____

_____

_____

_____

_____

_____

_____

_____

_____

_____

_____

_____

_____

_____

Today's Quote: "I don't know the key to success, but the key to failure is trying to please everybody." - Bill Cosby

Today's Question: Are you working to hard to please too many people?

_____

_____

_____

_____

_____

_____

_____

_____

_____

_____

_____

_____

_____

_____

_____

_____

_____

_____

Today's Quote: "Feelings make good advisers but poor masters." - Bill O'Hanlon

Today's Question: Are your feelings the main influence to your decisions?

_____

_____

_____

_____

_____

_____

_____

_____

_____

_____

_____

_____

_____

_____

_____

_____

_____

_____

May 6ᵗʰ

Today's Quote: "Relying on yourself is a lost art." - Frank Shorter

Today's Question: Can you truly rely on yourself?

_____

_____

_____

_____

_____

_____

_____

_____

_____

_____

_____

_____

_____

_____

_____

_____

_____

_____

Today's Quote: "I just want you to understand you can never get more than a 100%. So you give me 60% today, you can't give me a 140% tomorrow. If you give me 60% today, you leave 40% on the table. You'll never get it back." - John Wooden

Today's Question: What is your favorite quotation or saying?

_____

_____

_____

_____

_____

_____

_____

_____

_____

_____

_____

_____

_____

_____

_____

_____

_____

_____

Today's Quote: "It is better to sleep on things beforehand than lie awake about them afterward." - Baltasar Gracian

Today's Question: When has a little extra patience helped you out?

_____

_____

_____

_____

_____

_____

_____

_____

_____

_____

_____

_____

_____

_____

_____

_____

_____

_____

Today's Quote: "How my achievements mock me!" - William Shakespeare

Today's Question: Have any of you good deeds or solid successes ever come back to haunt you?

_____

_____

_____

_____

_____

_____

_____

_____

_____

_____

_____

_____

_____

_____

_____

_____

_____

_____

_____

Today's Quote: "I have never been especially impressed by the heroics of people who are convinced they are about to change the world. I am more awed by those who struggle to make one small difference after another." - Ellen Goodman

Today's Question: What small difference did you mother make in your life that made a big difference in you?

_____

_____

_____

_____

_____

_____

_____

_____

_____

_____

_____

_____

_____

_____

_____

_____

_____

Today's Quote: "An undefined problem has an infinite number of solutions."
- Robert A. Humphrey

Today's Question: Are you applying the right solution to the right problem?

_____

_____

_____

_____

_____

_____

_____

_____

_____

_____

_____

_____

_____

_____

_____

_____

_____

_____

Today's Quote: "I am not afraid of the pen, or the scaffold, or the sword. I will tell the truth wherever I please." - Mother Jones

Today's Question: Are you telling yourself the truth?

_____

_____

_____

_____

_____

_____

_____

_____

_____

_____

_____

_____

_____

_____

_____

_____

_____

_____

Today's Quote: "To have that sense of one's intrinsic worth . . . is potentially to have everything . . ." - Joan Didion

Today's Question: Are you sure of your own worth?

_____

_____

_____

_____

_____

_____

_____

_____

_____

_____

_____

_____

_____

_____

_____

_____

_____

_____

_____

Today's Quote: "The miracle is this - the more we share, the more we have." - Leonard Nimoy

Today's Question: Do you have a problem with sharing?

_____

_____

_____

_____

_____

_____

_____

_____

_____

_____

_____

_____

_____

_____

_____

_____

_____

_____

_____

Today's Quote: "Your theory is crazy, but it's not crazy enough to be true." - Niels Bohr

Today's Question: Is it you or is it them who is crazy?

_____

_____

_____

_____

_____

_____

_____

_____

_____

_____

_____

_____

_____

_____

_____

_____

_____

_____

_____

_____

Today's Quote: "The will to be stupid is a very powerful force, but there are always alternatives." - Lois McMaster Bujold

Today's Question: How do you stop yourself from making stupid mistakes?

_____

_____

_____

_____

_____

_____

_____

_____

_____

_____

_____

_____

_____

_____

_____

_____

_____

_____

_____

Today's Quote: "There is no need to go to India or anywhere else to find peace. You will find that deep place of silence right in your room, your garden or even your bathtub." - Elisabeth Kubler-Ross

Today's Question: Where do you go to find peace?

_____

_____

_____

_____

_____

_____

_____

_____

_____

_____

_____

_____

_____

_____

_____

_____

_____

_____

_____

Today's Quote: "Autobiography is an unrivaled vehicle for telling the truth about other people." - Philip Guedalla

Today's Question: How do you give someone a message they might not want to hear?

_____

_____

_____

_____

_____

_____

_____

_____

_____

_____

_____

_____

_____

_____

_____

_____

_____

_____

Today's Quote: "There are few nudities so objectionable as the naked truth." - Agnes Repplier

Today's Question: How well do you handle the truth when faced with it?

_____

_____

_____

_____

_____

_____

_____

_____

_____

_____

_____

_____

_____

_____

_____

_____

_____

_____

May 20th

Today's Quote: "There is a time for many words, and there is also a time for sleep." - Homer

Today's Question: Do you have a problem with taking a break?

_____

_____

_____

_____

_____

_____

_____

_____

_____

_____

_____

_____

_____

_____

_____

_____

_____

_____

May 21ˢᵗ

Today's Quote: "Don't be afraid of the answers. Be afraid of not asking the questions." - Jennifer Hudson

Today's Question: Are you receiving relevant answers to the questions you are asking?

_____

_____

_____

_____

_____

_____

_____

_____

_____

_____

_____

_____

_____

_____

_____

_____

_____

_____

Today's Quote: "It's harder to make something good when you can't curse all the time." - Tina Fey

Today's Question: How often do social norms and conventions slow down your personal progress?

_____

_____

_____

_____

_____

_____

_____

_____

_____

_____

_____

_____

_____

_____

_____

_____

_____

_____

Today's Quote: "The Romans would never have found time to conquer the world if they had been obliged first to learn Latin." - Heinrich Heine

Today's Question: When has not following conventional rules worked in your favor?

_____

_____

_____

_____

_____

_____

_____

_____

_____

_____

_____

_____

_____

_____

_____

_____

_____

_____

_____

Today's Quote: "Chance is always powerful. Let your hook be always cast; in the pool where you least expect it, there will be a fish." - Ovid

Today's Question: How much of your life do you leave up to chance?

_____

_____

_____

_____

_____

_____

_____

_____

_____

_____

_____

_____

_____

_____

_____

_____

_____

_____

Today's Quote: "Never try to reason the prejudice out of a man. It was not reasoned into him, and cannot be reasoned out." - Sydney Smith

Today's Question: Is there a difference in the way you manage your own prejudice as opposed to how you deal with prejudice in others?

_____

_____

_____

_____

_____

_____

_____

_____

_____

_____

_____

_____

_____

_____

_____

_____

_____

_____

Today's Quote: "Man has to suffer. When he has no real afflictions, he invents some." - Jose Marti

Today's Question: Do you create your own problems?

_____

_____

_____

_____

_____

_____

_____

_____

_____

_____

_____

_____

_____

_____

_____

_____

_____

Today's Quote: "Repetition does not transform a lie into a truth." - Franklin D. Roosevelt

Today's Question: What do you keep telling yourself that you know isn't true?

_____

_____

_____

_____

_____

_____

_____

_____

_____

_____

_____

_____

_____

_____

_____

_____

_____

_____

_____

Today's Quote: "You can learn as much - or more - from one glance at a private space as you can from hours of exposure to a public face." - Malcolm Gladwell

Today's Question: How different is your public persona from your private one?

_____

_____

_____

_____

_____

_____

_____

_____

_____

_____

_____

_____

_____

_____

_____

_____

_____

Today's Quote: "I do not think much of a man who is not wiser today than he was yesterday." - Abraham Lincoln

Today's Question: What did you learn today?

_____

_____

_____

_____

_____

_____

_____

_____

_____

_____

_____

_____

_____

_____

_____

_____

_____

_____

_____

Today's Quote: "If the fans don't wanna come out to the ballpark, no one can stop 'em." - Yogi Berra

Today's Question: How would you rank your power of persuasion?

_____

_____

_____

_____

_____

_____

_____

_____

_____

_____

_____

_____

_____

_____

_____

_____

_____

_____

_____

Today's Quote: "How little a thing can make us happy when we feel that we have earned it." - Mark Twain

Today's Question: Is it better to take a loss than it is to accept an undeserved or unearned win?

_____

_____

_____

_____

_____

_____

_____

_____

_____

_____

_____

_____

_____

_____

_____

_____

_____

_____

JUNE

Today's Quote: "Only two things are infinite, the universe and human stupidity, and I'm not sure about the former." - Albert Einstein

Today's Question: What are some of the really stupid things you have done that you could have prevented?

_____

_____

_____

_____

_____

_____

_____

_____

_____

_____

_____

_____

_____

_____

_____

_____

_____

_____

Today's Quote: "If there is no struggle, there is no progress." - Frederick Douglass

Today's Question: What struggles in your life have been key to your current success?

_____

_____

_____

_____

_____

_____

_____

_____

_____

_____

_____

_____

_____

_____

_____

_____

_____

_____

Today's Quote: "A person's a person, no matter how small." - Theodor 'Dr. Seuss' Geisel

Today's Question: Do you give the proper respect to everyone?

_____

_____

_____

_____

_____

_____

_____

_____

_____

_____

_____

_____

_____

_____

_____

_____

_____

_____

Today's Quote: "No matter how good you are, there's a lot of luck involved." - Reggie Miller

Today's Question: How much of your success can you attribute to a little bit of luck?

_____

_____

_____

_____

_____

_____

_____

_____

_____

_____

_____

_____

_____

_____

_____

_____

_____

_____

_____

Today's Quote: "To me success can only be achieved through repeated failure and introspection. In fact, success represents 1% of your work that results from the 99% that is called failure." - Soichiro Honda

Today's Question: Does a fear of failure keep you from obtaining true success?

_____

_____

_____

_____

_____

_____

_____

_____

_____

_____

_____

_____

_____

_____

_____

_____

_____

_____

Today's Quote: "Count no day lost in which you waited your turn, took only your share, and sought advantage over no one." - Robert Brault

Today's Question: What is the advantage of living your life as a good citizen?

_____

_____

_____

_____

_____

_____

_____

_____

_____

_____

_____

_____

_____

_____

_____

_____

_____

Today's Quote: "It is not giving children more that spoils them; it is giving them more to avoid confrontation." - John Gray

Today's Question: What do you do to avoid conflict?

_____

_____

_____

_____

_____

_____

_____

_____

_____

_____

_____

_____

_____

_____

_____

_____

_____

_____

Today's Quote: "One single grateful thought raised to heaven is the most perfect prayer." - G. E. Lessing

Today's Question: Do you take the time to show gratitude?

_____

_____

_____

_____

_____

_____

_____

_____

_____

_____

_____

_____

_____

_____

_____

_____

_____

_____

_____

Today's Quote: "It is not what you have lost, but what you have left that counts." - Harold Russell

Today's Question: In times of loss, do you count your blessings for what you still have?

_____

_____

_____

_____

_____

_____

_____

_____

_____

_____

_____

_____

_____

_____

_____

_____

Today's Quote: "I've done the calculation and your chances of winning the lottery are identical whether you play or not." - Fran Lebowitz

Today's Question: What would you gain if you were able to take more chances in your life?

_____

_____

_____

_____

_____

_____

_____

_____

_____

_____

_____

_____

_____

_____

_____

_____

_____

_____

Today's Quote: "Mistrust the man who finds everything good, the man who finds everything evil and still more the man who is indifferent to everything." - Johann K. Lavater

Today's Question: What steps do you take to maintain a balanced mind?

_____

_____

_____

_____

_____

_____

_____

_____

_____

_____

_____

_____

_____

_____

_____

_____

_____

_____

_____

Today's Quote: "You have to allow a certain amount of time in which you are doing nothing in order to have things occur to you, to let your mind think." - Mortimer Adler

Today's Question: Do you have the patience to wait for the things that are to come to you?

_____

_____

_____

_____

_____

_____

_____

_____

_____

_____

_____

_____

_____

_____

_____

_____

_____

_____

Today's Quote: "Quit now, you'll never make it. If you disregard this advice, you'll be halfway there." - David Zucker

Today's Question: When the going gets tough, what keeps you from giving up?

_____

_____

_____

_____

_____

_____

_____

_____

_____

_____

_____

_____

_____

_____

_____

_____

_____

_____

Today's Quote: "The odds against there being a bomb on a plane are a million to one, and against two bombs a million times a million to one. Next time you fly, cut the odds and take a bomb." - Benny Hill

Today's Question: Do you give up if the odds fall against your chances of winning?

_____

_____

_____

_____

_____

_____

_____

_____

_____

_____

_____

_____

_____

_____

_____

_____

_____

June 15th

Today's Quote: "One of the hardest tasks of leadership is understanding that you are not what you are, but what you're perceived to be by others." - Edward L. Flom

Today's Question: Are you willing to take the lead?

_____

_____

_____

_____

_____

_____

_____

_____

_____

_____

_____

_____

_____

_____

_____

_____

_____

_____

Today's Quote: "We are all salesmen every day of our lives. We are selling our ideas, our plans, our enthusiasms to those with whom we come in contact." - Charles M. Schwab

Today's Question: Are you winning the right clientele in the form of friends and acquaintances?

_____

_____

_____

_____

_____

_____

_____

_____

_____

_____

_____

_____

_____

_____

_____

_____

_____

Today's Quote: "I have three daughters and I find as a result I played King Lear almost without rehearsal" - Peter Ustinov

Today's Question: Do you take the time to rehearse for the grand events in your life?

_____

_____

_____

_____

_____

_____

_____

_____

_____

_____

_____

_____

_____

_____

_____

_____

_____

_____

Today's Quote: "The wisest men follow their own direction." - Euripides

Today's Question: Do you give advice good enough to follow it yourself?

Today's Quote: "Making good judgments when one has complete data, facts, and knowledge is not leadership - it's bookkeeping." - Dee Hock

Today's Question: What are you waiting for?

_____

_____

_____

_____

_____

_____

_____

_____

_____

_____

_____

_____

_____

_____

_____

_____

_____

_____

June 20th

Today's Quote: "Eliminate something superfluous from your life. Break a habit. Do something that makes you feel insecure." - Piero Ferrucci

Today's Question: How often do you step out of your comfort zone?

_____

_____

_____

_____

_____

_____

_____

_____

_____

_____

_____

_____

_____

_____

_____

_____

_____

_____

June 21st

Today's Quote: "The nice thing about standards is that there are so many of them to choose from." - Andrew S. Tanenbaum

Today's Question: Are you the person who defines your personal standard?

_____

_____

_____

_____

_____

_____

_____

_____

_____

_____

_____

_____

_____

_____

_____

_____

_____

_____

Today's Quote: "Death is more universal than life, everyone dies but not everyone lives." - Albie Sachs

Today's Question: What is missing to keep you from calling your life a 'life?'

_____

_____

_____

_____

_____

_____

_____

_____

_____

_____

_____

_____

_____

_____

_____

_____

_____

_____

_____

June 23rd

Today's Quote: "I don't know half of you half as well as I should like; and I like less than half of you half as well as you deserve." - J. R. R. Tolkien

Today's Question: Do you like the people you hang out with?

_____

_____

_____

_____

_____

_____

_____

_____

_____

_____

_____

_____

_____

_____

_____

_____

_____

_____

_____

Today's Quote: "To try to be better is to be better." - Charlotte Cushman

Today's Question: How hard are you really trying?

_____

_____

_____

_____

_____

_____

_____

_____

_____

_____

_____

_____

_____

_____

_____

_____

_____

_____

Today's Quote: "It is better to be prepared for an opportunity and not have one than to have an opportunity and not be prepared." - Whitney Young, Jr.

Today's Question: If your opportunity were to come knocking today, would you be afraid to answer the door?

_____

_____

_____

_____

_____

_____

_____

_____

_____

_____

_____

_____

_____

_____

_____

_____

_____

_____

Today's Quote: "The trick is to make sure you don't die waiting for prosperity to come." - Lee Iacocca

Today's Question: Are you spending your days sowing for prosperity or hoping to reap from the work of others?

_____

_____

_____

_____

_____

_____

_____

_____

_____

_____

_____

_____

_____

_____

_____

_____

Today's Quote: "The superior person's learning goes in his ear, attaches to his heart, expands to the end of his limbs, and is established in his actions. Even in his smallest word or slightest action, he sets an example." - Mencius

Today's Question: How much time do you set aside for continued learning?

_____

_____

_____

_____

_____

_____

_____

_____

_____

_____

_____

_____

_____

_____

_____

_____

_____

_____

Today's Quote: "You are accountable for what you do, and no one else is accountable." - Edith Martin

Today's Question: Are you living up to your own responsibility for yourself?

_____

_____

_____

_____

_____

_____

_____

_____

_____

_____

_____

_____

_____

_____

_____

_____

_____

_____

_____

Today's Quote: "Oh God, how do the world and heavens confine themselves, when our hearts tremble in their own barriers!" - Johann Wolfgang von Goethe

Today's Question: Is fear the largest barrier between you and success?

_____

_____

_____

_____

_____

_____

_____

_____

_____

_____

_____

_____

_____

_____

_____

_____

_____

_____

_____

_____

Today's Quote: "Never say more than is necessary." - Richard Brinsley Sheridan

Today's Question: Are you a capable manager of your economy of words?

_____

_____

_____

_____

_____

_____

_____

_____

_____

_____

_____

_____

_____

_____

_____

_____

_____

_____

_____

_____

JULY

Today's Quote: "I don't have too many bad days because I just don't let them happen. When I'm having one of those days, I'll just be like. 'I'm not going to let this be a bad day,' and I'll do everything I can to turn it around." - Matt Dallas

Today's Question: What simple changes do you need to make to assure you do not have a dreadful start to your day?

_____

_____

_____

_____

_____

_____

_____

_____

_____

_____

_____

_____

_____

_____

_____

_____

_____

Today's Quote: "Productivity is never an accident. It is always the result of a commitment to excellence, intelligent planning, and focused effort." - Paul J. Meyer

Today's Question: Have you found a happy medium between being a planner and a do'er?

_____

_____

_____

_____

_____

_____

_____

_____

_____

_____

_____

_____

_____

_____

_____

_____

_____

July 3rd

Today's Quote: "Give a little love to a child, and you get a great deal back."
- John Ruskin

Today's Question: What small investment offered you the greatest return when cashed in?

_____

_____

_____

_____

_____

_____

_____

_____

_____

_____

_____

_____

_____

_____

_____

_____

_____

Today's Quote: "Maybe the greatest challenge now is to find a way to keep independence while also committing ourselves to the ties that bind people, families, and ultimately societies together." - Jane O'Reilly

Today's Question: Are you claiming you own independence today?

_____

_____

_____

_____

_____

_____

_____

_____

_____

_____

_____

_____

_____

_____

_____

_____

_____

_____

Today's Quote: "Enjoy your own life without comparing it with that of another." - Marquis de Condorcet

Today's Question: Are you your own person?

_____

_____

_____

_____

_____

_____

_____

_____

_____

_____

_____

_____

_____

_____

_____

_____

_____

_____

Today's Quote: "Quality is not an act, it is a habit." - Aristotle

Today's Question: How long does it take for you to break in a new habit?

_____

_____

_____

_____

_____

_____

_____

_____

_____

_____

_____

_____

_____

_____

_____

_____

_____

_____

_____

Today's Quote: "The most violent element in society is ignorance." - Emma Goldman

Today's Question: Do you really believe that 'ignorance is bliss?'

_____

_____

_____

_____

_____

_____

_____

_____

_____

_____

_____

_____

_____

_____

_____

_____

_____

Today's Quote: "If you want to be respected, you must respect yourself." - Spanish Proverb

Today's Question: If you won't stand up for yourself, who do you expect to stand up for you?

_____

_____

_____

_____

_____

_____

_____

_____

_____

_____

_____

_____

_____

_____

_____

_____

_____

_____

Today's Quote: "Even with the best of maps and instruments, we can never fully chart our journeys." - Gail Pool

Today's Question: Can you enjoy the trip without having a firm destination?

_____

_____

_____

_____

_____

_____

_____

_____

_____

_____

_____

_____

_____

_____

_____

_____

_____

_____

_____

_____

Today's Quote: "In real life, events seem much less dramatic." - Jessica Savitch

Today's Question: What event in your life didn't happen that made you the success you are today?

_____

_____

_____

_____

_____

_____

_____

_____

_____

_____

_____

_____

_____

_____

_____

_____

_____

_____

Today's Quote: "We cannot direct the wind, but we can adjust the sails." - Bertha Calloway

Today's Question: Have you mastered the art of going with the flow?

_____

_____

_____

_____

_____

_____

_____

_____

_____

_____

_____

_____

_____

_____

_____

_____

_____

_____

Today's Quote: "When people keep telling you that you can't do a thing, you kind of like to try it." - Margaret Chase Smith

Today's Question: Do you tend to try harder because of the doubts of others?

_____

_____

_____

_____

_____

_____

_____

_____

_____

_____

_____

_____

_____

_____

_____

_____

_____

July 13th

Today's Quote: "Do or do not. There is no try." - Yoda

Today's Question: What is your biggest excuse for not succeeding?

_____

_____

_____

_____

_____

_____

_____

_____

_____

_____

_____

_____

_____

_____

_____

_____

_____

_____

Today's Quote: "He who every morning plans the transaction of the day and follows out that plan, carries a thread that will guide him through the maze of the most busy life. But where no plan is laid, where the disposal of time is surrendered merely to the chance of incidence, chaos will soon reign." - Victor Hugo

Today's Question: Is not keep a tight schedule keeping chaos in your life?

_____

_____

_____

_____

_____

_____

_____

_____

_____

_____

_____

_____

_____

_____

_____

_____

_____

Today's Quote: "No trumpets sound when the important decisions of our life are made. Destiny is made known silently." - Agnes de Mille

Today's Question: Are you struggling with making major decisions?

_____

_____

_____

_____

_____

_____

_____

_____

_____

_____

_____

_____

_____

_____

_____

_____

_____

_____

Today's Quote: "Dreaming permits each and every one of us to be quietly and safely insane every night of our lives." - Charles William Dement

Today's Question: Are you brave enough to share some of your crazier ideas?

_____

_____

_____

_____

_____

_____

_____

_____

_____

_____

_____

_____

_____

_____

_____

_____

_____

_____

_____

Today's Quote: "Anything not worth doing is worth not doing well. Think about it." - Elias Schwartz

Today's Question: What would happen if you stopped 'doing?'

_____

_____

_____

_____

_____

_____

_____

_____

_____

_____

_____

_____

_____

_____

_____

_____

_____

July 18th

Today's Quote: "The wisest mind has something yet to learn." - George Santayana

Today's Question: Have you reached your limit on learning?

_____

_____

_____

_____

_____

_____

_____

_____

_____

_____

_____

_____

_____

_____

_____

_____

_____

Today's Quote: "Too many times women try to be competitive with each other. We should help support each other, rather than try to be better than each other." - Katarina Witt

Today's Question: Are you working to better yourself or be better than those around you?

_____

_____

_____

_____

_____

_____

_____

_____

_____

_____

_____

_____

_____

_____

_____

_____

_____

_____

July 20th

Today's Quote: "That's one small step for [a] man, one giant leap for mankind" - Neil Armstrong

Today's Question: What will you do today that will go down in 'history?'

_____

_____

_____

_____

_____

_____

_____

_____

_____

_____

_____

_____

_____

_____

_____

_____

_____

_____

July 21ˢᵗ

Today's Quote: "We need men who can dream of things that never were." - John F. Kennedy

Today's Question: Can you 'see' your dreams before you start to work on making them come true?

_____

_____

_____

_____

_____

_____

_____

_____

_____

_____

_____

_____

_____

_____

_____

_____

_____

July 22nd

Today's Quote: "The great secret that all old people share is that you really haven't changed in 70 or 80 years. Your body changes, but you don't change at all." - Doris Lessing

Today's Question: Do you regard age as an enemy or a friend?

Today's Quote: "If you don't make mistakes, you're not working on hard enough problems. And that's a big mistake." - Frank Wilczek

Today's Question: Are you making enough mistakes?

_____

_____

_____

_____

_____

_____

_____

_____

_____

_____

_____

_____

_____

_____

_____

_____

_____

Today's Quote: "If our house be on fire, without inquiring whether it was fired from within or without, we must try to extinguish it." - Thomas Jefferson

Today's Question: Do you get so caught up in details that you can never properly act?

_____

_____

_____

_____

_____

_____

_____

_____

_____

_____

_____

_____

_____

_____

_____

_____

_____

_____

Today's Quote: "Insanity is often the logic of an accurate mind overtaxed." - Oliver Wendell Holmes

Today's Question: Do you need to take a break?

_____

_____

_____

_____

_____

_____

_____

_____

_____

_____

_____

_____

_____

_____

_____

_____

_____

_____

Today's Quote: "The second I stop laughing I know I'm beaten, and that's not about to happen." - Steve Errey

Today's Question: Have you ever stared down defeat?

_____

_____

_____

_____

_____

_____

_____

_____

_____

_____

_____

_____

_____

_____

_____

_____

_____

Today's Quote: "The game of life is the game of boomerangs. Our thoughts, deeds and words return to us sooner or later, with astounding accuracy." - Florence Shinn

Today's Question: Would you like to receive back the same thoughts and emotions you send out to the world?

_____

_____

_____

_____

_____

_____

_____

_____

_____

_____

_____

_____

_____

_____

_____

_____

_____

_____

Today's Quote: "Respect a man, he will do the more." - James Howell

Today's Question: Are you waiting to get respect before you give it in return?

_____

_____

_____

_____

_____

_____

_____

_____

_____

_____

_____

_____

_____

_____

_____

_____

_____

_____

Today's Quote: "Win as if you were used to it, lose as if you enjoyed it for a change" - Golnik Eric

Today's Question: Are you as respectful in winning as in losing?

_____

_____

_____

_____

_____

_____

_____

_____

_____

_____

_____

_____

_____

_____

_____

_____

_____

_____

Today's Quote: "You're never a loser until you quit trying." - Mike Ditka

Today's Question: At what point do you decide it's not worth the effort to fight anymore?

_____

_____

_____

_____

_____

_____

_____

_____

_____

_____

_____

_____

_____

_____

_____

_____

_____

_____

Today's Quote: "I am free of all prejudice. I hate everyone equally." - W. C. Fields

Today's Question: Do you have enough hate in your life?

_____

_____

_____

_____

_____

_____

_____

_____

_____

_____

_____

_____

_____

_____

_____

_____

_____

_____

AUGUST

Today's Quote: "Dying is a very dull, dreary affair. And my advice to you is to have nothing whatever to do with it." - W. Somerset Maugham

Today's Question: How do you determine if a person is dead on the inside?

_____

_____

_____

_____

_____

_____

_____

_____

_____

_____

_____

_____

_____

_____

_____

_____

_____

_____

August 2ⁿᵈ

Today's Quote: "I'm glad I don't have to explain to a man from Mars why each day I set fire to dozens of little pieces of paper, and then put them in my mouth." - Mignon McLaughlin

Today's Question: Do you feel compelled to continue performing outdated rituals?

_____

_____

_____

_____

_____

_____

_____

_____

_____

_____

_____

_____

_____

_____

_____

_____

_____

Today's Quote: "When the water reaches the upper level, follow the rats." - Claude Swanson

Today's Question: Are you ignoring signs of trouble?

_____

_____

_____

_____

_____

_____

_____

_____

_____

_____

_____

_____

_____

_____

_____

_____

_____

_____

Today's Quote: "We can change if we want to." - Denis Waitley

Today's Question: Do you really want to change?

_____

_____

_____

_____

_____

_____

_____

_____

_____

_____

_____

_____

_____

_____

_____

_____

_____

_____

August 5th

Today's Quote: "Waiting is a trap. There will always be reasons to wait. The truth is, there are only two things in life, reasons and results, and reasons simply don't count." - Dr. Robert Anthony

Today's Question: Is it really a good reason?

_____

_____

_____

_____

_____

_____

_____

_____

_____

_____

_____

_____

_____

_____

_____

_____

_____

_____

Today's Quote: "One doesn't discover new lands without consenting to lose sight of the shore for a very long time." - Andre Gide

Today's Question: Do you have an adventurer's spirit?

_____

_____

_____

_____

_____

_____

_____

_____

_____

_____

_____

_____

_____

_____

_____

_____

_____

_____

_____

Today's Quote: "I have a simple philosophy. Fill what's empty. Empty what's full. And scratch where it itches." - Alice Roosevelt Longworth

Today's Question: Are the simplest answers the best for the most complicated questions?

_____

_____

_____

_____

_____

_____

_____

_____

_____

_____

_____

_____

_____

_____

_____

_____

_____

Today's Quote: "Be to her virtues very kind. Be to her faults a little blind." - Matthew Prior

Today's Question: What do you choose to see in other people?

_____

_____

_____

_____

_____

_____

_____

_____

_____

_____

_____

_____

_____

_____

_____

_____

_____

_____

Today's Quote: "The last temptation is the greatest treason: to do the right deed for the wrong reason." - T. S. Eliot

Today's Question: Do others question your motives?

_____

_____

_____

_____

_____

_____

_____

_____

_____

_____

_____

_____

_____

_____

_____

_____

_____

_____

_____

Today's Quote: "Life is just a mirror, and what you see out there, you must first see inside of you." - Wally 'Famous' Amos

Today's Question: What image are you projecting to the world?

_____

_____

_____

_____

_____

_____

_____

_____

_____

_____

_____

_____

_____

_____

_____

_____

_____

_____

_____

Today's Quote: "Plans fail for lack of counsel, but with many advisers they succeed." - King Solomon

Today's Question: Are you listening?

_____

_____

_____

_____

_____

_____

_____

_____

_____

_____

_____

_____

_____

_____

_____

_____

_____

_____

Today's Quote: ". . . when you have eliminated the impossible, whatever remains, however improbable, must be the truth." - Sir Arthur Conan Doyle

Today's Question: Are you believing what you are seeing?

_____

_____

_____

_____

_____

_____

_____

_____

_____

_____

_____

_____

_____

_____

_____

_____

_____

_____

Today's Quote: "The people of hope are those who believe that God created them for a purpose and that He will provide for their needs as they seek to fulfill His purpose in their lives." - Pope John Paul II

Today's Question: Are you ignoring your purpose?

_____

_____

_____

_____

_____

_____

_____

_____

_____

_____

_____

_____

_____

_____

_____

_____

_____

_____

August 14th

Today's Quote: "I have always felt that the moment when first you wake up in the morning is the most wonderful of the twenty-four hours." - Monica Baldwin

Today's Question: Are you starting your day with a positive attitude?

_____

_____

_____

_____

_____

_____

_____

_____

_____

_____

_____

_____

_____

_____

_____

_____

_____

Today's Quote: "The greatest conflicts are not between two people but between one person and himself." - Garth Brooks

Today's Question: How do you resolve a conflict with yourself?

_____

_____

_____

_____

_____

_____

_____

_____

_____

_____

_____

_____

_____

_____

_____

_____

_____

_____

Today's Quote: "For a long time it seemed to me that real life was about to begin, but there was always some obstacle in the way. Something had to be got through first, some unfinished business; time still to be served, a debt to be paid. Then life would begin. At last it dawned on me that these obstacles were my life." - Bette Howland

Today's Question: Is now the right time to act?

_____

_____

_____

_____

_____

_____

_____

_____

_____

_____

_____

_____

_____

_____

_____

_____

Today's Quote: "When it's time to make a decision about a person or problem, trust your intuition (and) act." - Bud Hadfield

Today's Question: When faced with a problem or situation, can you 'trust your gut' when making a decision?

_____

_____

_____

_____

_____

_____

_____

_____

_____

_____

_____

_____

_____

_____

_____

_____

_____

Today's Quote: "Anybody can win unless there happens to be a second entry." - George Ade

Today's Question: What do you do to ensure a win for yourself?

_____

_____

_____

_____

_____

_____

_____

_____

_____

_____

_____

_____

_____

_____

_____

_____

_____

_____

_____

_____

Today's Quote: "Price is what you pay. Value is what you get." - Warren Buffett

Today's Question: Is it worth the price you pay?

_____

_____

_____

_____

_____

_____

_____

_____

_____

_____

_____

_____

_____

_____

_____

_____

_____

_____

_____

Today's Quote: "A lot of fellows nowadays have a B.A., M.D., or Ph.D. Unfortunately, they don't have a J.O.B." - Fats Domino

Today's Question: Does what you know help you or hurt you?

_____

_____

_____

_____

_____

_____

_____

_____

_____

_____

_____

_____

_____

_____

_____

_____

_____

_____

August 21st

Today's Quote: "It is well that war is so terrible - otherwise we would grow too fond of it." - Robert E. Lee

Today's Question: Are you falling in love with the pain in your life?

_____

_____

_____

_____

_____

_____

_____

_____

_____

_____

_____

_____

_____

_____

_____

_____

_____

_____

Today's Quote: "Many attempts to communicate are nullified by saying too much." - Robert Greenleaf

Today's Question: Are you talking too much?

_____

_____

_____

_____

_____

_____

_____

_____

_____

_____

_____

_____

_____

_____

_____

_____

_____

_____

_____

Today's Quote: "Associate with men of good quality if you esteem your own reputation; for it is better to be alone than in bad company." - George Washington

Today's Question: Who are you hanging out with?

_____

_____

_____

_____

_____

_____

_____

_____

_____

_____

_____

_____

_____

_____

_____

_____

_____

Today's Quote: "The pendulum will swing back." - Joseph G. Cannon

Today's Question: Do you prepare for the possible bad times while times are good?

_____

_____

_____

_____

_____

_____

_____

_____

_____

_____

_____

_____

_____

_____

_____

_____

_____

_____

Today's Quote: "It is our choices . . . that show what we truly are, far more than our abilities." - J. K. Rowling

Today's Question: Are you making the right choices?

_____

_____

_____

_____

_____

_____

_____

_____

_____

_____

_____

_____

_____

_____

_____

_____

_____

_____

Today's Quote: "There is no revenge so complete as forgiveness." - Josh Billings

Today's Question: Who do you need to forgive?

_____

_____

_____

_____

_____

_____

_____

_____

_____

_____

_____

_____

_____

_____

_____

_____

_____

_____

_____

Today's Quote: "The world is my classroom and every man is my teacher" - Myles Munroe

Today's Question: What did you learn today?

_____

_____

_____

_____

_____

_____

_____

_____

_____

_____

_____

_____

_____

_____

_____

_____

_____

Today's Quote: "Always render more and better service than is expected of you, no matter what your task may be." - Og Mandino

Today's Question: What is good service?

_____

_____

_____

_____

_____

_____

_____

_____

_____

_____

_____

_____

_____

_____

_____

_____

_____

_____

Today's Quote: "I am only one, but I am one. I cannot do everything, but I can do something. And I will not let what I cannot do interfere with what I can do." - Edward Everett Hale

Today's Question: Can one person really make a difference?

_____

_____

_____

_____

_____

_____

_____

_____

_____

_____

_____

_____

_____

_____

_____

_____

_____

_____

_____

August 30th

Today's Quote: "If you don't have enemies, you don't have character." - Paul Newman

Today's Question: Are you making enough enemies?

_____

_____

_____

_____

_____

_____

_____

_____

_____

_____

_____

_____

_____

_____

_____

_____

_____

_____

Today's Quote: "There are no great people in this world, only great challenges which ordinary people rise to meet." - William Frederick Halsey, Jr.

Today's Question: Are you prepared to rise to the occasion?

_____

_____

_____

_____

_____

_____

_____

_____

_____

_____

_____

_____

_____

_____

_____

_____

_____

_____

SEPTEMBER

Today's Quote: "Man's biggest mistake is to believe that he's working for someone else." - Nashua Cavalier

Today's Question: Do you work harder when you feel like you were working for yourself?

_____

_____

_____

_____

_____

_____

_____

_____

_____

_____

_____

_____

_____

_____

_____

_____

_____

September 2nd

Today's Quote: "I want to caution you against the idea that balance has to be a routine that looks the same week in and week out." - Kevin Thoman

Today's Question: What daily routine must you maintain in order keep your life in order?

_____

_____

_____

_____

_____

_____

_____

_____

_____

_____

_____

_____

_____

_____

_____

_____

_____

_____

_____

Today's Quote: "It's not whether you get knocked down; it's whether you get back up." - Vince Lombardi

Today's Question: How do you reset yourself after a setback?

_____

_____

_____

_____

_____

_____

_____

_____

_____

_____

_____

_____

_____

_____

_____

_____

_____

_____

Today's Quote: "If, before going to bed every night, you will tear a page from the calendar, and remark, "there goes another day of my life, never to return," you will become time conscious." - A. B. Zu Tavern

Today's Question: Are you truly conscious to how much time you are consuming?

Today's Quote: "You cannot prove your worth by bylines and busyness." - Katelyn S. Irons

Today's Question: Do you really need all the hustle and bustle for living a normal life?

_____

_____

_____

_____

_____

_____

_____

_____

_____

_____

_____

_____

_____

_____

_____

_____

_____

September 6th

Today's Quote: "Age wrinkles the body. Quitting wrinkles the soul." - Douglas MacArthur

Today's Question: What is your 'true' age?

_____

_____

_____

_____

_____

_____

_____

_____

_____

_____

_____

_____

_____

_____

_____

_____

_____

Today's Quote: "Any fool can make a rule, and any fool will mind it." - Henry David Thoreau

Today's Question: Are you a rule breaker?

_____

_____

_____

_____

_____

_____

_____

_____

_____

_____

_____

_____

_____

_____

_____

_____

_____

_____

Today's Quote: "Only I can change my life. No one can do it for me." - Carol Burnett

Today's Question: Why aren't you making that change right now?

_____

_____

_____

_____

_____

_____

_____

_____

_____

_____

_____

_____

_____

_____

_____

_____

_____

_____

Today's Quote: "Be thankful that you have a life, and forsake your vain and presumptuous desire for a second one." - Richard Dawkins

Today's Question: Are you pinning your hopes on a second chance at an opportunity?

_____

_____

_____

_____

_____

_____

_____

_____

_____

_____

_____

_____

_____

_____

_____

_____

_____

_____

Today's Quote: "The young have aspirations that never come to pass, the old have reminiscences of what never happened." - Saki

Today's Question: Do you remember things as they actually happened?

_____

_____

_____

_____

_____

_____

_____

_____

_____

_____

_____

_____

_____

_____

_____

_____

_____

September 11th

Today's Quote: "Any event, once it has occurred, can be made to appear inevitable by a competent historian." - Lee Simonson

Today's Question: What life events had to happen to put you where you are today?

_____

_____

_____

_____

_____

_____

_____

_____

_____

_____

_____

_____

_____

_____

_____

_____

_____

_____

September 12th

Today's Quote: "If the road is easy, you're likely going the wrong way." - Terry Goodkind

Today's Question: How can you tell if the opportunity is worth the adversity?

_____

_____

_____

_____

_____

_____

_____

_____

_____

_____

_____

_____

_____

_____

_____

_____

_____

_____

_____

September 13th

Today's Quote: "Derive happiness in oneself from a good day's work, from illuminating the fog that surrounds us." - Henri Matisse

Today's Question: Are you satisfied with the week that has passed?

_____

_____

_____

_____

_____

_____

_____

_____

_____

_____

_____

_____

_____

_____

_____

_____

_____

_____

Today's Quote: "Because he has never forgiven himself any fault, he can forgive no one else's." - Linda Berdoll

Today's Question: Are you ready to name your faults?

_____

_____

_____

_____

_____

_____

_____

_____

_____

_____

_____

_____

_____

_____

_____

_____

_____

_____

_____

Today's Quote: "If you accept the expectations of others, especially negative ones, then you never will change the outcome." - Michael Jordan

Today's Question: Who are you listening to?

_____

_____

_____

_____

_____

_____

_____

_____

_____

_____

_____

_____

_____

_____

_____

_____

_____

_____

September 16th

Today's Quote: "The heart sometimes doesn't care about limits." - Kristen Ashley

Today's Question: Do you know your limits?

_____

_____

_____

_____

_____

_____

_____

_____

_____

_____

_____

_____

_____

_____

_____

_____

_____

_____

Today's Quote: "It's kind of fun to do the impossible." - Walt Disney

Today's Question: What is your most improbable achievement?

_____

_____

_____

_____

_____

_____

_____

_____

_____

_____

_____

_____

_____

_____

_____

_____

_____

_____

_____

Today's Quote: "I speak Spanish to God, Italian to women, French to men, and German to my horse." - Charles V of France

Today's Question: Are you speaking the same language as those you are trying to communicate with?

_____

_____

_____

_____

_____

_____

_____

_____

_____

_____

_____

_____

_____

_____

_____

_____

_____

Today's Quote: "The undertaking of a new action brings new strength." - Evenius

Today's Question: Could you use a fresh start?

_____

_____

_____

_____

_____

_____

_____

_____

_____

_____

_____

_____

_____

_____

_____

_____

_____

_____

Today's Quote: "Observe your enemies, for they first find out your faults." - Antisthenes

Today's Question: What lessons can you learn from your detractors?

_____

_____

_____

_____

_____

_____

_____

_____

_____

_____

_____

_____

_____

_____

_____

_____

_____

_____

September 21ˢᵗ

Today's Quote: "Concentration comes out of a combination of confidence and hunger." - Arnold Palmer

Today's Question: What drives you to achieve more?

_____

_____

_____

_____

_____

_____

_____

_____

_____

_____

_____

_____

_____

_____

_____

_____

_____

Today's Quote: "I really do believe I can accomplish a great deal with a big grin, I know some people find that disconcerting, but that doesn't matter." - Beverly Sills

Today's Question: How would you rate your smile?

_____

_____

_____

_____

_____

_____

_____

_____

_____

_____

_____

_____

_____

_____

_____

_____

_____

_____

_____

Today's Quote: "Every day holds the possibility of a miracle." - Elizabeth David

Today's Question: Are you ready for your miracle?

_____

_____

_____

_____

_____

_____

_____

_____

_____

_____

_____

_____

_____

_____

_____

_____

_____

_____

September 24th

Today's Quote: "Laughter and tears are both responses to frustration and exhaustion. I myself prefer to laugh, since there is less cleaning up to do afterward." - Kurt Vonnegut

Today's Question: How do you handle frustration?

_____

_____

_____

_____

_____

_____

_____

_____

_____

_____

_____

_____

_____

_____

_____

_____

_____

_____

September 25th

Today's Quote: "The problem with human attraction is not knowing if it will be returned." - Becca Fitzpatrick

Today's Question: What are you attracting?

_____

_____

_____

_____

_____

_____

_____

_____

_____

_____

_____

_____

_____

_____

_____

_____

_____

Today's Quote: "You can't do anything about the length of your life, but you can do something about its width and depth." - Evan Esar

Today's Question: What gives your life meaning?

_____

_____

_____

_____

_____

_____

_____

_____

_____

_____

_____

_____

_____

_____

_____

_____

_____

_____

_____

Today's Quote: "A day without sunshine is like, you know, night." - Steve Martin

Today's Question: Are you ignoring the obvious?

_____

_____

_____

_____

_____

_____

_____

_____

_____

_____

_____

_____

_____

_____

_____

_____

_____

_____

Today's Quote: "You can go as far as you think, imagine and dream. Anything is possible." - Lailah Gifty Akita

Today's Question: What are you not doing that you should be doing spectacularly?

_____

_____

_____

_____

_____

_____

_____

_____

_____

_____

_____

_____

_____

_____

_____

_____

_____

_____

_____

Today's Quote: "It's a sad day when you find out that it's not accident or time or fortune, but just yourself that kept things from you." - Lillian Hellman

Today's Question: How would things be different if you were to get out of your own way?

_____

_____

_____

_____

_____

_____

_____

_____

_____

_____

_____

_____

_____

_____

_____

_____

_____

Today's Quote: "The people I distrust most are those who want to improve our lives but have only one course of action." - Frank Herbert

Today's Question: Do you apply a universal solution to everything?

_____

_____

_____

_____

_____

_____

_____

_____

_____

_____

_____

_____

_____

_____

_____

_____

_____

_____

_____

OCTOBER

Today's Quote: "No matter how love-sick a woman is, she shouldn't take the first pill that comes along." - Dr. Joyce Brothers

Today's Question: Are you overeager?

_____

_____

_____

_____

_____

_____

_____

_____

_____

_____

_____

_____

_____

_____

_____

_____

_____

_____

Today's Quote: "Use your imagination not to scare yourself to death but to inspire yourself to life." - Adele Brookman

Today's Question: Do you fear bad dreams?

_____

_____

_____

_____

_____

_____

_____

_____

_____

_____

_____

_____

_____

_____

_____

_____

_____

_____

Today's Quote: "If the best is possible, than good is never enough and only do the best." - Robert Siahaan

Today's Question: Can you handle not being the best of the best?

_____

_____

_____

_____

_____

_____

_____

_____

_____

_____

_____

_____

_____

_____

_____

_____

_____

_____

_____

Today's Quote: "An author is a fool who, not content with boring those he lives with, insists on boring future generations." - Charles de Montesquieu

Today's Question: What will future generations say about the life you lived?

_____

_____

_____

_____

_____

_____

_____

_____

_____

_____

_____

_____

_____

_____

_____

_____

_____

_____

_____

Today's Quote: "The hardest thing about the road not taken is that you never know where it might have led." - Lisa Wingate

Today's Question: Can you improve your future by making better decisions in the present?

_____

_____

_____

_____

_____

_____

_____

_____

_____

_____

_____

_____

_____

_____

_____

_____

_____

_____

Today's Quote: "We judge ourselves by what we feel capable of doing, while others judge us by what we have already done." - Henry Wadsworth Longfellow

Today's Question: Have you put in enough work to own a lasting legacy?

_____

_____

_____

_____

_____

_____

_____

_____

_____

_____

_____

_____

_____

_____

_____

_____

_____

_____

Today's Quote: "All I can say about life is, Oh God, enjoy it!" - Bob Newhart

Today's Question: What type of person can be opposed to having fun?

_____

_____

_____

_____

_____

_____

_____

_____

_____

_____

_____

_____

_____

_____

_____

_____

_____

_____

Today's Quote: "Never be afraid to speak your mind on relevant issues; good leaders stand for relevance and they are never afraid to face the facts head on. Bad leaders see the problems, close their eyes and do something else!" - Israelmore Ayivor

Today's Question: Are you afraid to face the facts?

_____

_____

_____

_____

_____

_____

_____

_____

_____

_____

_____

_____

_____

_____

_____

_____

Today's Quote: "Part of being a hero is knowing when you don't need to be one anymore." - Alan Moore

Today's Question: Do you know when to let people fend for themselves?

_____

_____

_____

_____

_____

_____

_____

_____

_____

_____

_____

_____

_____

_____

_____

_____

_____

_____

_____

Today's Quote: "The fear of death is more to be dreaded than death itself."
- Publilius Syrus

Today's Question: How can you prove that your fears are warranted?

_____

_____

_____

_____

_____

_____

_____

_____

_____

_____

_____

_____

_____

_____

_____

_____

_____

_____

_____

Today's Quote: "Life is what happens to you while you're busy making other plans." - Allen Saunders

Today's Question: How often do you get to stick to your plan?

_____

_____

_____

_____

_____

_____

_____

_____

_____

_____

_____

_____

_____

_____

_____

_____

_____

_____

Today's Quote: "When anger rises, think of the consequences." – Confucius

Today's Question: Do you take into account the unintended consequences?

_____

_____

_____

_____

_____

_____

_____

_____

_____

_____

_____

_____

_____

_____

_____

_____

_____

_____

_____

Today's Quote: "Any word you have to hunt for in a thesaurus is the wrong word. There are no exceptions to this rule." - Stephen King

Today's Question: Can you trust your own judgment?

_____

_____

_____

_____

_____

_____

_____

_____

_____

_____

_____

_____

_____

_____

_____

_____

_____

_____

Today's Quote: "Beauty is in the eye of the beholder and it may be necessary from time to time to give a stupid or misinformed beholder a black eye." - Miss Piggy

Today's Question: How do you handle your challengers?

_____

_____

_____

_____

_____

_____

_____

_____

_____

_____

_____

_____

_____

_____

_____

_____

_____

Today's Quote: "Maps encourage boldness. They're like cryptic love letters. They make anything seem possible." - Mark Jenkins

Today's Question: If you could have the directions for success in one area, what would it be?

_____

_____

_____

_____

_____

_____

_____

_____

_____

_____

_____

_____

_____

_____

_____

_____

_____

_____

October 16th

Today's Quote: "Literature is an occupation in which you have to keep proving your talent to people who have none." - Jules Renard

Today's Question: Are you being forced to produce mediocre work?

_____

_____

_____

_____

_____

_____

_____

_____

_____

_____

_____

_____

_____

_____

_____

_____

_____

_____

October 17th

Today's Quote: "The public will believe anything, so long as it is not founded on truth." - Edith Sitwell

Today's Question: What makes you accept what you know as truth?

_____

_____

_____

_____

_____

_____

_____

_____

_____

_____

_____

_____

_____

_____

_____

_____

_____

_____

October 18th

Today's Quote: "We do not have to see the beginning and the end of our lives, but we must close our eyes and live as if we didn't start or would never end." - Michael Bassey Johnson

Today's Question: How much importance do you put on the way you start?

_____

_____

_____

_____

_____

_____

_____

_____

_____

_____

_____

_____

_____

_____

_____

_____

_____

_____

Today's Quote: "I envy people who drink. At least they have something to blame everything on." - Oscar Levant

Today's Question: Who or what is really to blame?

_____

_____

_____

_____

_____

_____

_____

_____

_____

_____

_____

_____

_____

_____

_____

_____

_____

_____

October 20th

Today's Quote: "Humor is a rubber sword - it allows you to make a point without drawing blood." - Mary Hirsch

Today's Question: How healthy is your sense of humor?

_____

_____

_____

_____

_____

_____

_____

_____

_____

_____

_____

_____

_____

_____

_____

_____

_____

Today's Quote: "Fall down. Make a mess. Break something occasionally. Know that your mistakes are your own unique way of getting to where you need to be. And remember that the story is never over." - Conan O'Brien

Today's Question: Do you dread making mistakes?

_____

_____

_____

_____

_____

_____

_____

_____

_____

_____

_____

_____

_____

_____

_____

_____

_____

_____

October 22nd

Today's Quote: "Smiles reach the hard-to-reach places." - Steve Wilson

Today's Question: Why aren't you smiling?

_____

_____

_____

_____

_____

_____

_____

_____

_____

_____

_____

_____

_____

_____

_____

_____

_____

Today's Quote: "In the end, we will remember not the words of our enemies, but the silence of our friends." - Martin Luther King Jr.

Today's Question: Do your friends have you back?

_____

_____

_____

_____

_____

_____

_____

_____

_____

_____

_____

_____

_____

_____

_____

_____

_____

_____

Today's Quote: "You cannot shake hands with a clenched fist." - Indira Gandhi

Today's Question: Can you put set side your animosity for the sake of making peace?

_____

_____

_____

_____

_____

_____

_____

_____

_____

_____

_____

_____

_____

_____

_____

_____

_____

_____

_____

Today's Quote: "You don't just luck into things as much as you'd like to think you do. You build step by step, whether it's friendships or opportunities." - Barbara Bush

Today's Question: How well do you build yourself up before taking on a challenge?

_____

_____

_____

_____

_____

_____

_____

_____

_____

_____

_____

_____

_____

_____

_____

_____

Today's Quote: "The best index to a person's character is how he treats people who can't do him any good, and how he treats people who can't fight back." - Abigail Van Buren

Today's Question: Are people near you drawn to you or put off because of your character?

_____

_____

_____

_____

_____

_____

_____

_____

_____

_____

_____

_____

_____

_____

_____

_____

_____

Today's Quote: "You cannot live a perfect day without doing something for someone who will never be able to repay you." - John Wooden

Today's Question: How would you end a perfect day?

_____

_____

_____

_____

_____

_____

_____

_____

_____

_____

_____

_____

_____

_____

_____

_____

_____

_____

October 28th

Today's Quote: "Could you imagine how horrible things would be if we always told others how we felt? Life would be intolerably bearable." - Randy K. Milholland

Today's Question: How much truth goes into your honest conversations?

_____

_____

_____

_____

_____

_____

_____

_____

_____

_____

_____

_____

_____

_____

_____

_____

_____

October 29th

Today's Quote: "You must pray that the way be long, full of adventures and experiences." - Constantine P. Cavafy

Today's Question: Are you enjoying the ride?

_____

_____

_____

_____

_____

_____

_____

_____

_____

_____

_____

_____

_____

_____

_____

_____

_____

_____

Today's Quote: "People who don't have much get ugly about giving up the little they have left." - Andrew Vachss

Today's Question: What is it that you overvalue?

_____

_____

_____

_____

_____

_____

_____

_____

_____

_____

_____

_____

_____

_____

_____

_____

_____

_____

Today's Quote: "The closing years of life are like the end of a masquerade party when the masks are dropped." - Arthur Schopenhauer

Today's Question: What masks are you wearing?

_____

_____

_____

_____

_____

_____

_____

_____

_____

_____

_____

_____

_____

_____

_____

_____

_____

_____

NOVEMBER

Today's Quote: "If we get everything that we want, we will soon want nothing that we get." - Vernon Luchies

Today's Question: Is too much of a good thing really such a bad thing?

_____

_____

_____

_____

_____

_____

_____

_____

_____

_____

_____

_____

_____

_____

_____

_____

_____

_____

Today's Quote: "I'm not a natural leader. I'm too intellectual; I'm too abstract; I think too much." - Newt Gingrich

Today's Question: Does knowing your limitations keep you from being exploited by them?

_____

_____

_____

_____

_____

_____

_____

_____

_____

_____

_____

_____

_____

_____

_____

_____

_____

Today's Quote: "Sometimes the reader will decide something else than the author's intent; this is certainly true of attempts to empirically decipher reality." - John M. Ford

Today's Question: How well can you decipher what is not being said?

_____

_____

_____

_____

_____

_____

_____

_____

_____

_____

_____

_____

_____

_____

_____

_____

_____

Today's Quote: "The first step to getting the things you want out of life is this: Decide what you want." - Ben Stein

Today's Question: Do you know exactly what you want?

_____

_____

_____

_____

_____

_____

_____

_____

_____

_____

_____

_____

_____

_____

_____

_____

_____

_____

November 5th

Today's Quote: "The way you overcome shyness is to become so wrapped up in something that you forget to be afraid." - Lady Bird Johnson

Today's Question: What does shyness have to do with not being able to achieve awesome results?

_____

_____

_____

_____

_____

_____

_____

_____

_____

_____

_____

_____

_____

_____

_____

_____

_____

Today's Quote: "When men speak ill of thee, live so as nobody may believe them." - Plato

Today's Question: Do you run your life in a way that other people should believe what is being said about you?

_____

_____

_____

_____

_____

_____

_____

_____

_____

_____

_____

_____

_____

_____

_____

_____

November 7th

Today's Quote: "Meticulous planning will enable everything a man does to appear spontaneous." - Mark Caine

Today's Question: Do you confuse being spontaneous with being scattered and indecisive?

_____

_____

_____

_____

_____

_____

_____

_____

_____

_____

_____

_____

_____

_____

_____

_____

_____

Today's Quote: "You can't have everything . . . where would you put it?" - Stephen Wright

Today's Question: Where do your priorities lie?

_____

_____

_____

_____

_____

_____

_____

_____

_____

_____

_____

_____

_____

_____

_____

_____

_____

_____

Today's Quote: "It takes a lot of courage to show your dreams to someone else." - Erma Bombeck

Today's Question: Are you ashamed of your dreams?

_____

_____

_____

_____

_____

_____

_____

_____

_____

_____

_____

_____

_____

_____

_____

_____

_____

Today's Quote: "There is nothing wrong with America that cannot be cured by what is right with America." - Bill Clinton

Today's Question: Can the source of a problem be the source of the solution?

_____

_____

_____

_____

_____

_____

_____

_____

_____

_____

_____

_____

_____

_____

_____

_____

_____

_____

Today's Quote: "The inner fire is the most important thing mankind possesses." - Edith Sodergran

Today's Question: Have you surrendered your inner fire to the everyday schedule of your life?

_____

_____

_____

_____

_____

_____

_____

_____

_____

_____

_____

_____

_____

_____

_____

_____

_____

_____

November 12th

Today's Quote: "If you wish success in life, make perseverance your bosom friend, experience your wise counselor, caution your elder brother and hope your guardian genius." - Joseph Addison

Today's Question: Do you have a circle of friends that keep you grounded?

_____

_____

_____

_____

_____

_____

_____

_____

_____

_____

_____

_____

_____

_____

_____

_____

_____

Today's Quote: "The person who makes a success of living is the one who see his goal steadily and aims for it unswervingly. That is dedication." - Cecil B. DeMille

Today's Question: Do you make setting goals a priority in your life?

_____

_____

_____

_____

_____

_____

_____

_____

_____

_____

_____

_____

_____

_____

_____

_____

November 14th

Today's Quote: "If you do not tell the truth about yourself you cannot tell it about other people." - Virginia Woolf

Today's Question: Are you as honest with others as you are with yourself?

_____

_____

_____

_____

_____

_____

_____

_____

_____

_____

_____

_____

_____

_____

_____

_____

_____

Today's Quote: "If people only knew how hard I work to gain my mastery, it wouldn't seem so wonderful at all." - Michelangelo

Today's Question: Do people know the true amount of effort you put into your successes?

_____

_____

_____

_____

_____

_____

_____

_____

_____

_____

_____

_____

_____

_____

_____

_____

_____

_____

Today's Quote: "You create your opportunities by asking for them." - Patty
Hansen

Today's Question: Do you ask for opportunities?

_____

_____

_____

_____

_____

_____

_____

_____

_____

_____

_____

_____

_____

_____

_____

_____

_____

_____

Today's Quote: "Here is a test to find whether your mission on earth is finished: If you are alive, it isn't." - Richard Bach

Today's Question: Do you know what your mission in life should be?

_____

_____

_____

_____

_____

_____

_____

_____

_____

_____

_____

_____

_____

_____

_____

_____

_____

_____

Today's Quote: "If you don't like your present address change it. You're not a tree!" - Jim Rohn

Today's Question: Do you feel like you can't shake off your problems and move on?

_____

_____

_____

_____

_____

_____

_____

_____

_____

_____

_____

_____

_____

_____

_____

_____

_____

_____

Today's Quote: "In prosperity our friends know us; in adversity we know our friends." - John Churton Collins

Today's Question: Would your friends stick with you if you lost everything?

_____

_____

_____

_____

_____

_____

_____

_____

_____

_____

_____

_____

_____

_____

_____

_____

November 20th

Today's Quote: "When you're climbing the ladder of life, you go rung by rung, one step at a time. Don't look too far up, set your goals high but take one step at a time. Sometimes you don't think you're progressing until you step back and see how high you've really gone." - Donny Osmond

Today's Question: Are you happy with the way your life is going?

_____

_____

_____

_____

_____

_____

_____

_____

_____

_____

_____

_____

_____

_____

_____

_____

Today's Quote: "Life has no limitations, except the ones you make." - Les Brown

Today's Question: What are the biggest limitations you put on yourself?

_____

_____

_____

_____

_____

_____

_____

_____

_____

_____

_____

_____

_____

_____

_____

_____

_____

_____

Today's Quote: "The Indian knew how to live without wants, to suffer without complaint, and to die singing." - Alexis de Tocqueville

Today's Question: Are you a complainer?

_____

_____

_____

_____

_____

_____

_____

_____

_____

_____

_____

_____

_____

_____

_____

_____

_____

Today's Quote: "Never give a child a sword." - Latin Proverb

Today's Question: How often do you ignore good advice?

_____

_____

_____

_____

_____

_____

_____

_____

_____

_____

_____

_____

_____

_____

_____

_____

_____

_____

_____

Today's Quote: "Happy are those who dream dreams and are ready to pay the price to make them come true." - Leon Suenens

Today's Question: How much is it worth to you?

_____

_____

_____

_____

_____

_____

_____

_____

_____

_____

_____

_____

_____

_____

_____

_____

_____

_____

Today's Quote: "The world stands aside to let anyone pass who knows where he is going." - David Starr Jordan

Today's Question: Do you know where you are going?

_____

_____

_____

_____

_____

_____

_____

_____

_____

_____

_____

_____

_____

_____

_____

_____

_____

Today's Quote: "Setting a good example is a far better way to spread ideals than through force of arms." - Ron Paul

Today's Question: Are you living up to the example you are trying to set?

_____

_____

_____

_____

_____

_____

_____

_____

_____

_____

_____

_____

_____

_____

_____

_____

_____

_____

November 27th

Today's Quote: "Success is to be measured not so much by the position that one has reached in life as by the obstacles which he has overcome." - Booker T. Washington

Today's Question: What obstacles have you had to overcome lately?

_____

_____

_____

_____

_____

_____

_____

_____

_____

_____

_____

_____

_____

_____

_____

_____

_____

Today's Quote: "Temptation rarely comes in working hours. It is in their leisure time that men are made or marred." - W. N. Taylor

Today's Question: How do you stay alert?

_____

_____

_____

_____

_____

_____

_____

_____

_____

_____

_____

_____

_____

_____

_____

_____

_____

Today's Quote: "The art of war is simple enough. Find out where your enemy is. Get at him as soon as you can. Strike him as hard as you can, and keep moving on." - Ulysses S. Grant

Today's Question: Do you have problems following simple directions?

_____

_____

_____

_____

_____

_____

_____

_____

_____

_____

_____

_____

_____

_____

_____

_____

_____

_____

Today's Quote: "It is possible to store the mind with a million facts and still be entirely uneducated." - Alec Bourne

Today's Question: Do you know what you really know?

_____

_____

_____

_____

_____

_____

_____

_____

_____

_____

_____

_____

_____

_____

_____

_____

_____

_____

_____

_____

DECEMBER

Today's Quote: " The thing that is really hard, and really amazing, is giving up on being perfect and beginning the work of becoming yourself." - Anna Quindlen

Today's Question: How much will you really give up by giving up?

_____

_____

_____

_____

_____

_____

_____

_____

_____

_____

_____

_____

_____

_____

_____

_____

_____

_____

Today's Quote: "When you are kind to someone in trouble, you hope they'll remember and be kind to someone else. And it'll become like a wildfire." - Whoopi Goldberg

Today's Question: Are you making an effort to spread good cheer?

_____

_____

_____

_____

_____

_____

_____

_____

_____

_____

_____

_____

_____

_____

_____

_____

_____

_____

Today's Quote: "If one morning I walked on top of the water across the Potomac River, the headline that afternoon would read 'President Can't Swim'." - Lyndon B. Johnson

Today's Question: Are you telling the whole story?

_____

_____

_____

_____

_____

_____

_____

_____

_____

_____

_____

_____

_____

_____

_____

_____

_____

_____

Today's Quote: "I get a lot of cracks about my hair, mostly from men who don't have any." - Ann Richards

Today's Question: Can you maintain a healthy jealousy?

_____

_____

_____

_____

_____

_____

_____

_____

_____

_____

_____

_____

_____

_____

_____

_____

_____

_____

December 5th

Today's Quote: "Acts of sacrifice and decency without regard to what's in it for you create ripple effects. Ones that lift up families and communities, that spread opportunity and boost our economy." - Barack Obama

Today's Question: How much more satisfaction could you receive if you worked for no reward?

_____

_____

_____

_____

_____

_____

_____

_____

_____

_____

_____

_____

_____

_____

_____

_____

_____

_____

Today's Quote: "Better shun the bait, than struggle in the snare." - John Dryden

Today's Question: Are you gullible?

_____

_____

_____

_____

_____

_____

_____

_____

_____

_____

_____

_____

_____

_____

_____

_____

_____

_____

_____

Today's Quote: "Pain makes man think. Thought makes man wise. Wisdom makes life endurable." - John Patrick

Today's Question: Are you gaining something from your troubles?

_____

_____

_____

_____

_____

_____

_____

_____

_____

_____

_____

_____

_____

_____

_____

_____

_____

_____

_____

Today's Quote: "All you need in this life is ignorance and confidence; then success is sure." - Mark Twain

Today's Question: What is your acceptable failure rate?

_____

_____

_____

_____

_____

_____

_____

_____

_____

_____

_____

_____

_____

_____

_____

_____

_____

_____

_____

Today's Quote: "We all have the extraordinary coded within us, waiting to be released." - Jean Houston

Today's Question: What are you waiting on?

_____

_____

_____

_____

_____

_____

_____

_____

_____

_____

_____

_____

_____

_____

_____

_____

_____

_____

Today's Quote: "People don't want their lives fixed. Nobody wants their problems solved. Their dramas. Their distractions. Their stories resolved. Their messes cleaned up. Because what would they have left? Just the big scary unknown." - Chuck Palahniuk

Today's Question: What is distracting you from getting things done?

_____

_____

_____

_____

_____

_____

_____

_____

_____

_____

_____

_____

_____

_____

_____

_____

_____

Today's Quote: "No one who cannot rejoice in the discovery of his own mistakes deserves to be called a scholar." - Donald Foster

Today's Question: Are you okay with the mistakes you make?

_____

_____

_____

_____

_____

_____

_____

_____

_____

_____

_____

_____

_____

_____

_____

_____

_____

_____

Today's Quote: "When I'm writing a book, sentence by sentence, I'm not thinking theoretically. I'm just trying to work out the story from inside the characters I've got." - Salman Rushdie

Today's Question: Are you playing the wrong character in the story of your life?

_____

_____

_____

_____

_____

_____

_____

_____

_____

_____

_____

_____

_____

_____

_____

_____

_____

Today's Quote: "The more we do, the more we can do; the more busy we are the more leisure we have." - William Hazlitt

Today's Question: Can you gain productivity from productivity?

_____

_____

_____

_____

_____

_____

_____

_____

_____

_____

_____

_____

_____

_____

_____

_____

_____

_____

Today's Quote: "Miracles don't just happen, people make them happen" - Misato Katsuragi

Today's Question: Are you working on your own miracles?

_____

_____

_____

_____

_____

_____

_____

_____

_____

_____

_____

_____

_____

_____

_____

_____

_____

_____

Today's Quote: "I am not an adventurer by choice but by fate." - Vincent van Gogh

Today's Question: Are you on a path of your own choosing?

_____

_____

_____

_____

_____

_____

_____

_____

_____

_____

_____

_____

_____

_____

_____

_____

_____

Today's Quote: "Selecting the right person for the right job is the largest part of coaching." - Philip Crosby

Today's Question: How good at you at 'coaching up?'

_____

_____

_____

_____

_____

_____

_____

_____

_____

_____

_____

_____

_____

_____

_____

_____

_____

_____

Today's Quote: "There are well-dressed foolish ideas just as there are well-dressed fools." - Nicolas Chamfort

Today's Question: How good are your ideas?

_____

_____

_____

_____

_____

_____

_____

_____

_____

_____

_____

_____

_____

_____

_____

_____

_____

_____

Today's Quote: "There's no such thing as coulda, shoulda, or woulda. If you shoulda and coulda, you woulda done it." - Pat Riley

Today's Question: Do you have a reoccurring excuse for not getting something done?

_____

_____

_____

_____

_____

_____

_____

_____

_____

_____

_____

_____

_____

_____

_____

_____

_____

_____

December 19th

Today's Quote: "I do not know beneath what sky nor on what seas shall be thy fate; I only know it shall be high, I only know it shall be great." - Richard Hovey

Today's Question: Are you enjoying the journey to success?

_____

_____

_____

_____

_____

_____

_____

_____

_____

_____

_____

_____

_____

_____

_____

_____

_____

Today's Quote: "A test of what is real is that it is hard and rough. Joys are found in it, not pleasure. What is pleasant belongs to dreams." - Simone Weil

Today's Question: Do you equate 'happy' with 'easy?'

_____

_____

_____

_____

_____

_____

_____

_____

_____

_____

_____

_____

_____

_____

_____

_____

_____

_____

Today's Quote: "People who know the most, know they know so little, while people who know nothing want to take all day to tell it to you." - Charlie "Tremendous" Jones

Today's Question: Where do you get your knowledge?

_____

_____

_____

_____

_____

_____

_____

_____

_____

_____

_____

_____

_____

_____

_____

_____

_____

_____

December 22nd

Today's Quote: "As for ourselves, yes, we must be meek, bear injustice, malice, rash judgment. We must turn the other cheek, give up our cloak, go a second mile." - Dorothy Day

Today's Question: Do your snap judgments usually lead you down the right or wrong path?

_____

_____

_____

_____

_____

_____

_____

_____

_____

_____

_____

_____

_____

_____

_____

_____

Today's Quote: "You have to do what you love to do, not get stuck in that comfort zone. Life is not a dress rehearsal. This is it." - Lucinda Basset

Today's Question: Are you enjoying your life?

_____

_____

_____

_____

_____

_____

_____

_____

_____

_____

_____

_____

_____

_____

_____

_____

_____

_____

December 24th

Today's Quote: "What worries you masters you." - Haddon W. Robinson

Today's Question: Do you let your fears drive your life?

_____

_____

_____

_____

_____

_____

_____

_____

_____

_____

_____

_____

_____

_____

_____

_____

_____

_____

Today's Quote: "Challenges are gifts that force us to search for a new center of gravity. Don't fight them. Just find a different way to stand." - Oprah Winfrey

Today's Question: What do you do with your gifts?

_____

_____

_____

_____

_____

_____

_____

_____

_____

_____

_____

_____

_____

_____

_____

_____

_____

Today's Quote: "If you do not wish to be prone to anger, do not feed the habit; give it nothing which may tend to its increase." - Epictetus

Today's Question: Why can't you just let go of a grudge?

_____

_____

_____

_____

_____

_____

_____

_____

_____

_____

_____

_____

_____

_____

_____

_____

_____

_____

Today's Quote: "My pitching philosophy is simple - keep the ball way from the bat." - Satchel Paige

Today's Question: Are you making the process more complicated than it needs to be?

_____

_____

_____

_____

_____

_____

_____

_____

_____

_____

_____

_____

_____

_____

_____

_____

Today's Quote: "If you had started doing anything two weeks ago, by today you would have been two weeks better at it." - John Mayer

Today's Question: Are you truly dedicated to your work?

_____

_____

_____

_____

_____

_____

_____

_____

_____

_____

_____

_____

_____

_____

_____

_____

_____

_____

Today's Quote: "Acceptance is not submission; it is acknowledgment of the facts of a situation. Then deciding what you're going to do about it." - Kathleen Casey Theisen

Today's Question: Are there times when it would be wiser to choose to live in denial?

_____

_____

_____

_____

_____

_____

_____

_____

_____

_____

_____

_____

_____

_____

_____

_____

_____

Today's Quote: "Even if you're on the right track, you'll get run over if you just sit there." - Will Rogers

Today's Question: Are you content being the person you are right now?

_____

_____

_____

_____

_____

_____

_____

_____

_____

_____

_____

_____

_____

_____

_____

_____

_____

_____

December 31ˢᵗ

Today's Quote: "One of the secrets of success is to refuse to let temporary setbacks defeat us." - Mary Kay

Today's Question: Do you see your setbacks as stone walls or stepping stones?

_____

_____

_____

_____

_____

_____

_____

_____

_____

_____

_____

_____

_____

_____

_____

_____

_____

_____

ABOUT J CLEVELAND PAYNE

J Cleveland Payne has taken his obsession with the news and notes of the day and drive to gain more knowledge on leadership an personal improvement to form a growing media following, powered in part by the seemingly need for constantly updated information in the internet age. As a very early participant in the world of 'new media,' Payne has produced top ranking Internet creations such as newsletters and podcast, while also producing award winning products for traditional mediums of television, radio, and printed books.

Payne's list of *is's* is extensive: Air Force Veteran, M.B.A., fitness instructor, news producer and reporter, radio talk show host, radio program director, television producer and master control operator, entrepreneur, public speaker, business and personal development consultant, podcaster, internet magazine editor, blogger, and published author. The roles he is most proud of is being the husband to Kristina, father to Alex and Johanna, and uncle to Jalia and Christian.

AVAILABLE NOW: WELCOME TO YOUR MONDAY

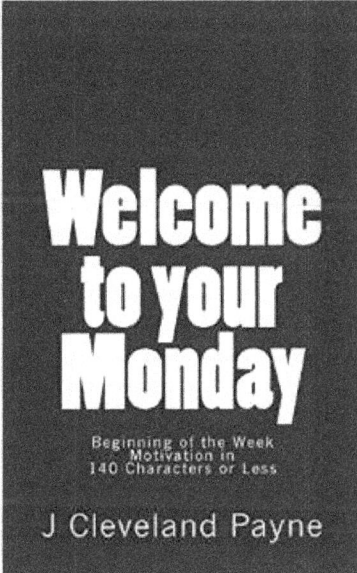

The Amazon Kindle Best Seller That Puts A Year's Worth Of Quick Motivational Messages In The Palm Of Your Hand

Visit

j.mp/welcometoyourmonday

or search for

'Welcome to your Monday'

at Amazon.com

One tweet sent in late 2012. It began with 'Welcome to your Monday.' It was followed by 115 more characters. One tweet sent and just like that, J Cleveland Payne had created a new motivational series in a new style he was unfamiliar with: extremely short and to the point. That challenge would be on he would happily accept, turning longer maxim of wisdom and insight into short and pithy bites that were easy to take and take in. The Welcome to Your Monday Twitter series is billed as 'Monday morning motivation in 140 characters or less,' and this book offers up the first years' worth of Monday's past. While the occasional epiphany is available for you to claim, most of these thoughts and ideas will just remind you of what you already should be doing or reaffirm that what you are doing is the right thing. Very little will be found to be original or earth-shattering thoughts. The author is very okay with that.

AVAILABLE NOW: SO FORTY HAPPENED

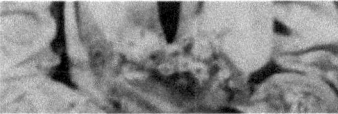

In an attempt to clear a real milestone after a few years of setbacks and backslides, J Cleveland Payne began an all-out attempt to produce a decent book he could present as a memoir for the first 40 years of his life. You can be the judge of whether this book is truly worthy of being graded as 'decent,' but Payne did succeed in producing a book, and triumphantly hit is target of being released before his 40th birthday on September 29th, 2014. In this chronicle the mind of a man trying to reach a milestone, Payne offers up his true feelings of his past struggles and regrets, along with admitting to some obvious personal issues. He reveals some uncertainty he has for whatever time he may have left while sharing the joys and struggles of fatherhood with a virtual adult and an actual toddler. In the process of weaving tales with a lot more woe than expected, but some general moments of joy and wonder.

www.ingramcontent.com/pod-product-compliance
Lightning Source LLC
Chambersburg PA
CBHW070905100426
42737CB00047B/2617